ιction

Radio programme production

a manual for training

by Richard Aspinall

Unesco

Published by the United Nations
Educational, Scientific and Cultural Organization
Place de Fontenoy, 75700 Paris
First edition 1971
Second impression 1973
Third impression 1977
Composed by Imprimerie-Reliure Maison Mame, Tours
Printed by Imprimerie Roby, Arcueil

ISBN 92-3-101030-1

Preface

Broadcasting plays an important part in the communication process which is essential to development, for it is concerned with the transmission and use of knowledge and information which bring greater numbers of the society into the mainstream of national life. Particularly since the introduction of the mass-produced transistor, opportunities for communicating with vast new audiences—the great majority of people without whose involvement 'development' is not possible—have been multiplied many thousand times. The problems connected with the operation of radio stations in developing countries however are not solely technological. The best transmitting equipment, the finest broadcasting studios, render no service if they are not staffed adequately by qualified engineers, technicians, journalists and producers. The training of radio personnel therefore is a real necessity.

Over the years, Unesco has tried to help African States gradually solve their problems of training radio staff. While fellowships are being awarded for studies abroad, it is now generally recognized that training and particularly basic training should be provided within the countries concerned. Local training, however, is handicapped by the lack of a suitable training manual, as has so often been pointed out by specialists in the field. It is to these that the present book is expected to be of the greatest help, while their students may also find it useful. It is an attempt to provide a manual on radio production which reflects the special circumstances and requirements of training in developing countries.

The author, Richard Aspinall, has worked as a broadcasting instructor in Africa for many years and is now (1970) a radio training specialist at the Institute of Communication, University of Lagos (Nigeria).

The manual was commissioned following an Africa-wide study of broadcasting training needs and resources made on behalf of Unesco by two African radio and television professionals, Francis Bebey (Cameroon) and Alex Quarmyne (Ghana). Their report guided its approach and it has been scrutinized by them. Responsibility for the presentation and the views expressed rests with Mr. Aspinall.

While the background is Africa and the manual is primarily designed for radio instructors in that continent, it is hoped that the approach will commend itself to instructors and students in other parts of the world where radio is the prime medium of mass communication and a basic tool of development.

How to use this book

This book is intended to serve a number of purposes:

For those concerned in management, it provides ideas about the use of radio in Africa and a guide to the development of staff and staff training programmes.

For instructors and training officers, it offers source material for lectures and demonstrations and help in working out training projects. In the early chapters many questions are raised which can be used as the basis of class discussions. Discussion of ideas is valuable: it stimulates thinking and gives the instructor a chance to find out whether his ideas are getting through.

For senior producers who may have trainees to supervise but little time to spend with them, this book may provide what is needed for assignment work. It will be useful also for working broadcasters with little or no access to training facilities and for students of broadcasting it provides a course manual.

Outside contributors interested in radio, teachers and discussion group leaders can learn from it something about how radio and radio programming works.

If you are a student of broadcasting, we suggest that you form the habit of keeping notebooks. Keep one as a personal pronouncing dictionary in which you can enter new words as you learn their pronunciations and one as a translation dictionary for translating ideas into your own language. A third should be kept as an ideas and notes file—over the years this will become a valuable source of material for future broadcasts.

Contents

Part I   What is broadcasting all about?

I   The beginning and growth of radio

Incident at sea

For most of the ship's crew it was like any other day at sea. Routine duties on the long haul across the watery wilderness of the North Atlantic.

In the wireless cabin aft of the wheel-house, a stuffy cabin heavy with the acrid smells of battery acid and electric sparks, a young man sat writing out a fair copy of the shipping and weather information he had just received. He still wore his headphones although the regular transmission had closed some minutes ago. For him too it was a routine day. But suddenly there was a crackle in his headphones and a man's voice began speaking. The young operator dropped his pencil in his excitement. A voice by wireless? Incredible! But there was more to come. When the voice stopped speaking a violin started playing. The young man could hardly believe his ears. All he had ever heard before had been the rhythmical stutter of the dots and dashes of the morse code.

That young man was one of the very few listeners, all of them wireless operators at sea, to hear the first broadcast of entertainment ever made. It came from a transmitter on the American coast several hundred miles away. Some operator there had connected a telephone to his sending equipment and arranged a short programme. Whether he did this for fun or as a serious experiment we do not know, but his action certainly foreshadowed the birth of broadcasting.

Wireless telegraphy—that is wireless communication in coded pulses—was then in its infancy. It had been invented not long before by the Italian, Guglielmo Marconi. It was used at the time only for the point-to-point exchange of messages between ships at sea and the shore.

Background to the incident atsea

Marconi was one of the many inventors and scientists whose work during the nineteenth century brought about a revolution in communications. It was a tremendously inventive century—the locomotive, the telegraph and telephone, photography and moving pictures, the motor car and the aero-plane, the gramophone and magnetic recording, radio and even the picture tube on which we see television today all had their beginnings in that time.

The names of several of the pioneers have entered the folklore of modern electronics and are in daily use in every radio workshop: the Frenchman, *Amp*ère; the Americans, Bell (the deci*Bel*) and *Morse*; the British, *Fara*day and *Watt*; the Germans, *Hertz* and *Ohm*; and the Italian, *Volt*a. The works of these men in science and technology have helped to make life richer for all of us, and in broadcasting we owe them a special debt.

The development of the technical means of broadcasting came about as a result of the drive throughout the nineteenth century to solve some of the problems arising from the Industrial Revolution. The great expansion of manufacturing which followed it had created a hunger for more and more raw materials, wider markets, and faster methods of exchanging commercial infor-mation. The traditional techniques of communication were outmoded. The horse and cart could no longer carry the heavy burden of industry and the message runner could not keep up with the times.

There were attractive profits to be made by the men who could be first to solve some of these problems. Early in the nineteenth century many attempts were made to use the newly discovered phenomenon of electricity for cross-country signalling. A museum-full of oddities was invented but the most practical means was devised by Samuel Morse in 1835 using interrupted pulses of electricity in the form of a code. The idea rapidly took hold and in a very few years networks of telegraph wires on wooden poles spread across Europe, America and India. Soon cables were laid under the sea, even across the great width of the Atlantic Ocean. Great and costly quantities of wire cable were used. Then came more poles and more wire as the telephone made its appearance.

As the wired web of the telegraph spread farther and farther afield another idea excited the minds of the experimenters, wire-less telegraphy and telephony. Signals were sent through the waters of rivers and the earth itself but they failed to travel any great distance. Slowly the idea developed of using the air, aerial telegraphy. Towards the end of the century the thought occupied many scientists and experimenters but it was the young Marconi, at the age of 22, who proved that it was practical. In 1896 he sent his first wire-less message and he soon convinced hard-headed naval officers and merchant shipowners in Britain that it could work over long distances. As the new century opened he sent the morse letter 's' (. . .) across the 3,000 miles of the Atlantic—convincing proof, if any were needed, of the worth of aerial tele-graphy. In 1907 researchers in America and Germany showed that radio waves could be made to carry speech and other sounds, so paving the way to radio telephony and with it the possibility of broadcasting.

The beginning of radio

The use of wireless for popular broadcasting was a consequence of the world war of 1914–18. The fighting services needed improved equipment and large numbers of wireless operators; hundreds of thousands of men were trained in wireless signalling. It was these men who on their return to civil life led the demand for broadcasting services.

The demand was voiced against the background of greatly changed social conditions which followed the war. The bitter experience of the first modern war had given the man-in-the-street a new awareness of his political importance. He learnt that he must participate more in government if he was to prevent a recurrence of the catastrophe and therefore he had a right to information. The recent appearance of popular newspapers was a sign of the times and it was reasonable to expect that wireless too could play a part in the process of mass communication.

But the potential of broadcasting was discovered by accident.

One day in 1916 engineers of a manufacturing company in Pittsburgh (United States), were conducting experimental voice transmissions when they decided to alternate talking with music from gramophone records. They found to their surprise that they had many unexpected listeners—amateurs who were using home-built equipment. These amateurs were so pleased by the music that they wrote asking for more. Regular broadcasting began not long afterwards. The station was later licensed as KDKA, the world's first, and for several years the world's only, broadcasting station. It is still on the air.

At the end of the war ex-service signallers in many countries formed clubs to press for broadcasting services. They were supported by manufacturers who wanted to find peacetime uses for the techniques they had learnt in war. Governments slowly yielded and by the early 1920s broadcasting began in many lands. One manufacturer described the receiver as 'radio's magic music box'—a term soon popularized as 'radio'.

Growth

Early radio was very much a novelty for listeners and broadcasters alike. There was an element of excitement and adventure about it which even today marks the best of broadcasting, for radio is essentially a fun-game no matter how serious or important the programme material.

The early receiving sets were bulky and difficult to tune; the loudspeaker had not been invented and listening was limited to headphones. The studios were converted offices draped with heavy curtains; there were no mixing panels, no magnetic microphones, no electrical pick-ups and certainly no tape recording. The microphones had to be shaken before use, like a bottle of medicine. Gramophone records were played by acoustic gramophones in front of an open microphone. All other performances were live.

One of the tasks facing early broadcasters was to popularize radio listening and this had a great effect upon subsequent programming. Radio receivers were expensive—far more so than transistor sets today. If people were to be persuaded to buy them, the programmes needed to have a very wide popular appeal and so music and general entertainment were strongly featured. Talks and discussions were the highlights and they were prominently billed. There were no educational programmes nor were there programmes for special audiences, except sports fans. News was broadcast usually only late in the evening after the final editions of city newspapers had been sold because newspapers were the main source of news and they feared the competition of radio.

But despite the difficulties radio steadily grew. As technical progress was made more ambitious programmes became possible; dramas, newsreels and documentaries began to displace much of the music. The spread of land-line networks and the development of long distance short-wave broadcasting were important advances which brought scattered and distant communities into a kind of radio city and exposed them to metropolitan ideas. As more and more people listened to radio it began to have a powerful influence on public taste and on the shaping of public opinion.

These are some of the aspects of broadcasting which we shall examine as they are relevant to the role of broadcasting in developing countries.

Ownership and control

One of the questions arising from the introduction of broadcasting was: Who should own and operate such facilities? The question is pertinent even today in some countries where radio has now been long established. It is a good question for general consideration and in particular for discussion amongst students of broadcasting.

Should broadcasting facilities be owned and operated directly by the State as a department of government?

Should they be State-owned but their operation entrusted to professional broadcasters over whom the State has no direct control?

Should broadcasting be a private undertaking operated for personal or corporate profits in a similar way to a newspaper?

The general question was considered at length in the early days. There were fears that the radio-frequency spectrum would become overcrowded, leaving no room for military use. There was also uncertainty as to the probable social and political influence of radio. In the end many different systems were adopted in different parts of the world and from them have been derived most of the systems in use today.

In the United States the system most favoured was private ownership subject to licensing and broad general regulation by government. It led to a very rapid growth and the United States is today the most radio-conscious country in the world, with one radio station for every 32,000 listeners and more sets than people.

An early idea popular in Europe was user-ownership and societies and clubs were formed to finance and operate stations. Receiving sets tuned to fixed frequencies were made available to members. The system was not really practical as pirate listening could not be prevented. However, radio societies allied to approved political, religious or cultural groups still operate in some countries.

But although the societies failed as a whole they did give rise to the idea of statutory broadcasting corporations being established by government but independent of it to a greater or lesser degree. The system has subsequently been widely adopted and it works particularly well where the corporations are not dependent upon government for revenue.

Outright government ownership was also popular in Europe, although in some cases it was vested not in the central government but in provincial governments. The system led to the development of inter-regional programme exchanges—a development later adopted by the statutory corporations.

In Australia and Canada where broadcasting began quite early two systems grew up side by side. Private stations with considerable freedom were licensed by government which then itself went into competition with them. There are variations on this system, one being that a national authority has two outlets, one commercial and the other non-commercial.

Private broadcasting generally is financed by advertising whereas the statutory corporation system usually collects its revenue from licence fees. The costs of government broadcasting are borne out of general revenue, licences or a combination of both.

Many factors have shaped each country's choice, among them national traditions, political objectives and the amount of funds available. A more recent factor in developing countries has been the part assigned to broadcasting in the attainment of national objectives; this has weighed heavily in favour of a single authority integrating its programmes with other activities of government.

Another aspect of the relation of broadcasting to government is international. As broadcasting stations multiplied, some regional and international agreements were necessary to reduce the incidence of interference. The world body concerned with this is the International Telecommunication Union. There are also a number of regional and other groups concerned with programme exchange and general co-operation: the Asian Broadcasting Union, the Union African National Radio and Television Organizations, the European Broadcasting Union and the International Organization of Radio and Television (Eastern Europe).

Projects—class discussion

This chapter has given a broad outline of the general background of broadcasting. It can be used in several aspects of staff training. The following are discussion topics:

1. Broadcasting began in industrial countries at a time when the man-in-the-street wanted to have a larger share in government. Is this true to any extent of the beginning of radio in your own country?

2. There are several systems of ownership and control of broadcasting. What are their relative merits? Which is likely to lead to the most effective broadcasting?

3. Do you agree with the statement that broadcasting is essentially a 'fun-game'?

Action projects

These can be used as a later basis for talks exercises:

1. Find out what you can about the beginnings of broadcasting in your own country. What kind of service did it offer? What were its early programmes and hours of transmission? What audience did it serve? How was it and is it related to government? What international and regional groups does it belong to, and what are the functions of these groups?

2. What do you know of the work and the times of the scientists and experimenters mentioned in this chapter?

2   Mass communication

Radio broadcasting is one of several means of getting a message to a large number of people at the same time. This kind of communication is called mass communication, and radio, television, the cinema and newspapers are known as mass communication media.

The mass communication media are important to modern social processes; they bring public issues before wider forums than they can be reached by public meetings or through parliaments. They help to broaden our enjoyment of life and further our knowledge and understanding of things about us, and by bringing us information they help to stimulate individual and group action. In developing countries they have a significant role to play in speeding the process of social change.

In terms of general availability radio is the leading medium of mass communication. In much of the world, including most Asian and African countries, there are more radio sets than copies of daily newspapers, television sets or cinema seats. Radio has the further advantage of being comparatively inexpensive to operate once the initial capital outlay has been made for transmitters and receivers.

But, like all the mass media, radio has strengths and weaknesses. It is important to understand what these are if we are to make the most effective use of it.

Radio—its strengths

In a sense radio is universal. It can leap across distances and jump the barriers of illiteracy. We do not have to live close to a city to enjoy its benefits nor do we need to be able to read to understand it. We need not even speak the language to enjoy music by radio.

It has an immediacy which other media do not have to quite the same degree. Not only can it bring us today's news today, but today's news while it is happening. This characteristic it shares with television although the staging of a television news bulletin or the setting up of a television outside broadcast takes longer. Where the technical facilities exist radio can also talk with its listeners by telephone, thus putting members of an audience in touch with one another.

Radio is flexible. A scheduled programme can be dropped at short notice and replaced with something more topical or more urgent.

These are radio's principal strengths. It is universal, immediate, flexible and can be programmed comparatively inexpensively.

Radio—its weaknesses

But radio is dependent upon sound alone. Unfortunately what we only hear usually has less impact upon us than what we both hear and see.

Because radio is a sound-only medium we must be able to hear accurately and well if we are to profit from it. The language used must be within the listeners' understanding and the signal must be reliable and clear.

The quality of sound in the studio and at the receiver must be of the highest. Poor quality sound, muffled, distorted or confused, can tire listeners and lead to loss of interest. This is not just a technical consideration to be left to engineers; it concerns the producer as well, and the conscientious producer gives consideration to the conditions in which his programme is likely to be heard. A schools broadcast, for example, can be lost on children if the signal is hard to hear or if the schoolroom produces echoes or when it rains on an iron roof.

The other weakness of radio is that its messages are passing. If we fail to get the message the first time then the chances are we shall miss it altogether. We can read a newspaper or a book several times and we can go back to the cinema but, if we have missed a broadcast or failed to understand, it's unlikely that we'll have a second chance.

Turning weakness into strength

Sounds heard and overheard—provided they are interesting or provoking—can excite curiosity and stimulate the imagination to a very high degree. Story-tellers and troubadours the world over have known this for a very long time. By stimulating curiosity and imagination as spurs to learning radio can give good support to certain educational projects. The curiosity which sound excites accounts for the success of radio drama, whether the commonplace serial or the poetic drama of fine words and music.

Although sound-only appears at first to be a weakness there is much to be said in its favour. We are inclined to regard the things we hear only with far greater detachment than the things we both hear and see. We become less emotionally involved with radio than when we are watching television or films both of which can absorb us completely and often without stimulating thought. Again, while listening to the radio we can do other things. A radio discussion followed by music creates favourable conditions for family or group discussion of the theme of the programme: this is not true of the cinema and seldom of television.

So the radio link between broadcaster and audience may not be as weak as it at first appears. And it can be made much stronger by encouraging in listeners the habit of listening.

Radio lends itself extremely well to habit listening—that is tuning in to the same station every day of the week at the same time. It is the mainspring of its popularity.

Strength of personality

Radio is above all a vehicle for projecting personality and it is through personalities that it attracts and holds an audience.

Personality is hard to define. It is an invisible quality which attracts us to some people more than to others. It is this kind of person that radio should always seek for microphone work because personalities build audiences.

Many factors go into making a radio personality—voice, mannerisms, identification with the listener, the things he says and the way he says them. Publicity plays a part too, and once found a personality should be built up at every opportunity by personal public appearances on national or other important occasions, and through newspapers and magazines.

A radio personality need not be a learned person; material can always be prepared and written for him by others. If he has the kind of vibrant personality which attracts people, that is all that is needed; the rest is in the hands of his producer.

Good personalities heard throughout the day in every phase of programme activity give a station a personality of its own and help win and hold audiences for the more serious business of broadcasting.

Station image

The personality of a station is sometimes referred to as its image. It is the responsibility of the programme manager, programme controller or director of programmes—whatever his title—to design and build the station image.

This image, like human personality, is the sum total of many things and equally hard to define. The kind of music a station plays, the over-all quality of its sound, its general programming, its integrity in news reporting, its approach to its audience, its identification with its listeners and the microphone personalities it uses are all part of the station's image.

It is important for public service broadcasters in developing countries to understand the value of a station's image. Failure to develop a good station image can account for the popularity of foreign stations and the sizeable inroads they make on local audiences. Only when a station has developed a popular image can it start tackling general social problems and begin to play a leading role in national development.

Something needs to be said here about the over-use of outside contributors who may be little known beyond their own professional circles. They may be worthy men or women who have much to contribute to the general good, but unless they are personalities in themselves who can do something to build a station's image they may cost more listeners than they win. The erudite approach which they are inclined to adopt may not be the best method of contributing their ideas; they may communicate more effectively if their ideas are projected through established popular station personalities.

Similarly, minority programmes broadcast during mass listening times may damage the all-round station image. The minority programme catering to specialized sophisticated audiences is a luxury which can only be afforded by broadcasting organizations having control over more than one outlet. Through careful planning, however, some of this material can be fitted into general programming without damaging the station image.

The importance of personalities and the station image cannot be too strongly stressed. It is through the use of personalities that radio can gain the large audience without which it cannot claim to be a true medium of mass communication. Once established with its listeners, a station can begin to lead them into educational and specialist programming.

Radio and its audience

The more we know about an audience the better we are able to serve it. It is essential in good broadcasting to know exactly for whom each programme is intended. We must know the size of the audience, the listeners' attitudes and general outlook, what they think and feel, where they live, and perhaps even how much they earn, before we can begin to make programmes which will satisfy their needs.

Audience research is a specialized branch of broadcasting, but every programme maker needs to know something about his audience and the audience reaction to his programmes. Without this kind of information he may waste time and money and also fail in his primary purpose of communication.

There are well-established techniques for audience surveying but they are for the most part beyond the economic capability of a developing country. They are of two kinds: quantitative surveys and qualitative surveys.

The quantitative survey sets out to determine how many sets are tuned in to a particular station at various hours throughout the day each day of the week. It gives statistical information in percentages of sets in use, and it indicates the relative popularity of a station and its various programmes. These surveys are expensive and therefore rare in developing countries, although some have been conducted by foreign broadcasters and advertising agencies who have special interests in the relative popularity of various media.

On the other hand the qualitative survey, which tells something about how a programme is being accepted by its audience, can be done in a realistic way on a modest scale.

Qualitative surveying of a kind takes place whenever we are given an opinion on a programme through a letter from a listener or face to face, although we should beware of the opinions of friends who try to please us!

The basic technique of the qualitative survey is to organize listening panels representing listeners who have common interests in, say, music, drama, talks, news and so forth, and who come from widely differing cultural, educational, social and economic backgrounds. The panels may be paper-panels answering reply-paid questionnaires or they may be flesh-and-blood panels visited by station liaison staff. By polling these panels from time to time on specific programmes we can learn much about the audience reaction to them and whether or not the message is getting through.

This type of survey began with listeners' clubs set up in connexion with children's and women's programmes. Members were given inexpensive badges or illuminated certificates to encourage them to join and, incidentally, to advertise radio. Such surveys are still useful where stations cater for organized groups of listeners, for example teachers and radio rural forums.[1]

Qualitative surveys organized in conjunction with universities make good projects for students in several faculties. The preparation of questionnaires requires great skill in order to uncover the information really desired.

A useful and inexpensive way of learning something about the audience and its response to programmes is through the 'listeners' letters' type of programme. A provocative programme of this kind handled by a leading station personality who solicits opinions about programmes can reveal useful information. A careful analysis of the letters will bring to light many facts about their authors—educational and ethnic background, sex, age, community standing, place of residence in addition to their reactions to programmes. Sampling of this kind must be accepted for what it is, namely the response of literate listeners only who can afford to pay the postage and are interested enough to write—but even this is better than nothing.

Projects—class discussion

In this chapter it has been said that radio is above all a vehicle for projecting personality. Emphasis has been given to the use of personalities and the general development of the personality of the station. Do you agree:
1. That personalities should be used in every phase of programming?
2. That a station needs to be popular with its listeners in order to be able to communicate effectively with them?

Action projects

For students: Choose two stations, your own and another which you can hear well, and prepare short profiles of their images. Pay attention to the overall sound, the prevailing character of the music they play, the appeal

1. For useful questionnaires relating to rural radio forums see *An African Experiment in Radio Forums for Rural Development*, Paris, Unesco, 1968 (Reports and Papers in Mass Communication, 51).

which their announcers and other station personalities have for you, the general emphasis of their programming (talk or music, heavily public service or popular entertainment). If you prefer one to the other try to explain why.

For classes: Conduct two experiments in listening to two speech programmes, one having good sound quality and one having poor sound quality. Try to determine at which point class interest tends to stray. Discuss good and bad sound quality with the class.

Conduct a survey into a programme broadcast by your station. Enlist the aid of (a) its producer and obtain from him a clear statement regarding the audience for whom it is intended and any relevant material, such as letters from listeners indicating their reactions; (b) your station's propagation engineer and have him explain transmission coverage areas—is the audience within the primary coverage area? As a class project prepare a questionnaire about the programme and have each student conduct at least two interviews with listeners. Analyse the results: did the programme succeed with its intended audience?

3   Classification of programmes

In the very early days of radio the hours of transmission were short—in some cases as little as half an hour a week!—and the programmes were almost entirely music. As the hours increased talks were added and later on the news. It was not until technical facilities had greatly improved and audiences had grown in size that the elaborate programme structure of today emerged with its aim to please everybody.

The early patterns of programming were arrived at more by accident than design as no one had prior experience of the medium. They have had a profound effect on broadcasting and they continue to do so. As radio spread throughout the world there was a tendency to follow the patterns laid down by the pioneers with very little real questioning of how the medium could or should be used. This is in many ways unfortunate.

Before we discuss the use of radio we must first classify our programmes.

It is common practice in most broadcasting organizations to classify programmes under two general headings:

1. Spoken word broadcasting, which includes talks, discussions, educational broadcasting, programmes for special audiences (women, children, rural listeners), drama, documentary, magazines and news, and religious broadcasting.
2. Music, which includes programmes of gramophone records, live musical performances of all kinds and variety entertainment.

In recent years some broadcasting organizations have—perhaps more realistically—reclassified their programming as entertainment and current or community affairs. Under these newer headings there is more opportunity for the movement of programme staff and in consequence a better opportunity for the release of talent. Rigid departmentalizing of programme staff can destroy the initiative of the creative programme makers upon whom broadcasting depends.

The organization of production

The management of programmes of all categories is under the control of a programme manager (sometimes styled controller or director of programmes),

25

while the programmes are made under his direction by producers (sometimes known as directors, presentation assistants, programme or production assistants).

The programme manager is, in effect, the chief producer of a station, as it is his function to draw up the general programme plan, devise programme policy and provide leadership for his producers and help them to find and develop ideas. He needs to be extremely well versed in programming, with considerable practical experience as an active producer. The programme manager has a number of other special assistants working for him: an officer concerned with budget control, another with copyright control, another with over-all studio management of the technical facilities of production and the management of announcers.

The programme manager, his executive staff, the producers and their contributors, and the technical operators concerned in programme production all together make up the production team.

In some kinds of programming, such as educational broadcasting to schools and radio club broadcasting of the rural radio forum type, the team may have outside supporting officers called liaison officers whose work is to organize listening groups and report back to the programme manager or the producer concerned.

At many stations the programme manager organizes regular weekly staff meetings where all matters concerned with programmes are discussed; these meetings also give him a chance to see that programming follows the general policy he has laid down. They provide, too, a valuable training opportunity as they can be used for the auditioning and discussion of programmes. Where a station's programming is closely related to the over-all national objective they also help to keep station staff informed. Officers of various government departments and commissions can be invited to address the staff on the work of their departments and the discussions which follow often help broadcasters to relate their work more closely to the over-all national plan.

The programme structure

Radio programmes are not broadcast haphazard but according to a programme plan. The plan usually covers a three-month period and is broken down into a daily schedule. The balance of programmes within the daily schedule, that is the amount of time given to various categories of programmes and the time at which they are broadcast, is known as the programme structure.

The programme structure of a station and the way it is built up sets the station's character or image. The amount of time it gives to music, the kind of music it plays, the prominence or otherwise that it gives to news and educational broadcasting are all aspects of the programme structure of a radio station.

In broad terms the usual programme structure begins the day with bright music and frequent news bulletins and news summaries. Around 09.00 h the tempo of programming slows down and the morning hours cater for women's interests. News and informational material are the customary fare from 12.00 to 15.00 h. There is then generally a lull in programming until about 17.00 h when programmes of interest to children are broadcast. Evening programming picks up around 18.00 or 19.00 h and schedules are heavy with production features until about 22.00 h when most stations begin broadcasting popular music until they close down.

This is the pattern of radio programming which was set in the early days and is still followed to a very great extent in many countries. However, in countries where television has made inroads on radio's audiences, in recent years many stations have dropped feature programming and increased their output of popular music.

The important question, then, is whether the conventional programme structure is properly suited to developing countries. Are listeners' habits there the same as they are or were in the older radio countries?

When radio came to many countries in Africa and Asia it came as a service to the expatriate colonial communities. The programmes broadcast and the programme structures closely paralleled those they had known 'at home'. Even when the control of broadcasting passed into local hands the programme structures tended to remain the same, or if they did change the change was seldom significant. Educational schools broadcasting was sometimes added, where a station could afford it, and the character of music altered with the inclusion of more national music.

At about the time when many African countries became independent another significant development occurred which has tended to change the whole radio situation. The transistor receiver made its appearance. Unlike the older valve radios the transistor set was comparatively inexpensive and it could operate away from a mains electricity supply. Its appearance made possible a kind of democratization of radio listening. Whereas radio services had been virtually restricted to urban communities and mostly to well-to-do householders, the transistor brought radio services to almost everyone.

Yet despite this markedly changed situation, on the whole programmes continued to be cast in their imported moulds and to cater for the more sophisticated urban household listener. Even today, although this class of urban listener is possibly in the minority, a great deal of programme time is till devoted to him and programme structures appear to be designed largely with him alone in view.

Any original, creative approach to the use of radio in African and Asian countries must necessarily take into account this changed radio situation.

The uses of radio

Within limits radio can persuade and effectively influence large audiences, thereby contributing substantially to the thinking of a nation. There are many examples of this, some of the more beneficial being the influence of BBC radio upon spoken English and the appreciation of classical music built up by ABC radio in Australia.

Can this 'power' of radio be used to promote and support the cause of nation building in the developing countries?

Experimental radio clubs (the rural radio forums) in India and Ghana have produced ample evidence that it can. Radio clubs formed in rural communities have laid a ground plan of action for the use of radio in the cause of village welfare and betterment. Programmes have been specially devised for them in consultation with government officers and with the clubs themselves. The Indian experiment showed impressive gains in knowledge and it was found that the forum could become an important institution in village life both as a decision-making body to speed up common pursuits and as a means of forming a broadly based village democracy.

All the developing countries without exception are engaged in large undertakings in national development. They have embarked upon extensive education schemes and projects for rural improvement, and are establishing new and active medical health services, new industries. They are undergoing great changes with all the restlessness and social and political tensions which change inevitably brings. Situations are arising, therefore, in which radio should play an active part in speeding the process of change and making it understandable and acceptable.

Thus a new and particularly African use for radio begins to emerge: radio harnessed to the cause of national development and reflecting it in nearly every aspect of its programming. It is not the radio of the more advanced countries but a more vital radio of real meaning and use in the life of its listeners. It is not a radio that just talks about national development but participates in it through programmes which instruct and teach and inform from daybreak to well after dark.

African peoples have long been used to receiving oral instruction. They have for centuries heard the village-crier, the chant of the drum and songs of praise. They have a traditional experience which has better prepared them for radio than almost any other people in recent times. Effective programming should take into account the traditional techniques of communication in Africa and apply them to modern radio. In applying both the old and the new techniques radio has an outstanding use in Africa.

It remains only to seek out the real needs of listeners and to identify which aspects of national developmental planning are related to those needs; then both factors must be borne in mind in radio programming. This means developing a closely integrated pattern of programming whereby radio becomes the handmaiden of social welfare.

The responsibility of the broadcaster

Programme managers and producers in Africa face a tremendous challenge. The skilled broadcaster, well trained in his craft, can make a significant contribution to the development of his nation. He needs only to ask himself, at each stage of his programme work, how can I use radio in the best national interest?

In answering this question at his work he will really discover what broadcasting is all about.

Action projects

1. Classify the programmes of your station by name in the two categories given in this chapter, then re-classify them under the other two headings of entertainment and community affairs.
2. Draw a tree showing the programme organization of your station.
3. Explain in a few short lines why you took up broadcasting as a career.

Discussion project

1. Analyse the programme structure of your station and discuss with the class whether or not it is suitable to the habits of your listeners, and whether or not it is designed to meet their real needs. Could you design a more suitable structure? What new programmes would you put into it which are not there now?
2. What do you think of the idea of integrating the work of your station with the work of government departments concerned with social welfare? Can this be done without loss of independence for the broadcaster?

Part II   Technical facilities

4   The broadcast chain

Radio programme making is unavoidably a technical craft. It calls for a special way of developing ideas, a special approach to writing and a technique for translating ideas and scripts into workable radio terms. Familiarity with the technical facilities for production and knowledge of their operation is an essential part of the training of a radio producer. This is particularly necessary for more complex production work or where senior technical staff is scarce, as is often the case on small stations and in developing countries.

Before examining the facilities for production we must understand in outline the process of programme transmission.

When we speak or strike a drum or make any kind of sound we cause the air about us to vibrate and a series of invisible waves of energy is set up. These waves are made by the vibration of our vocal cords or the skin of the drum or the vibration of whatever is making the sound. If it is a low-pitched sound, then the vibrations are slow; if it is high-pitched the vibrations are fast. The word 'frequency' is used to describe the speed of the vibrations which is measured in cycles per second, also called Hertz. The terms kilocycles or kiloHertz and megacycles or megaHertz are used for thousands and millions of cycles per second.

There is an exact relationship between the speed of vibration or frequency and the length of the pressure wave which it produces. You can demonstrate this for yourself the next time you shave or wash. Gently paddle a finger in the hand-basin and watch the ripples on the surface of the water. By paddling slowly you set up widely spaced long waves, measuring from crest to crest, while by paddling rapidly the spaces between the ripples become less and the wavelengths shorter.

When we speak before a microphone the energy of the sound or acoustic wave acts upon it to produce an alternating current of electrical energy. This current has very little pressure, therefore its voltage is raised by amplifiers in the control room. It then passes as an electric current, alternating at the frequency of the sound waves, along telephone wires to the transmitter.

At the transmitter, high-powered oscillators produce steady waves of radio energy and send them into the aerial system. These radio waves have high frequencies ranging from 150 kiloHertz to 100 megaHertz; the choice of frequency, and therefore the wavelength of the station in metres is determined by the purpose which the station serves. The lower frequency long and medium waves are used where the broadcast has to travel only a few hundred miles while higher frequency short and ultra-short waves are used where it has to travel several hundreds or thousands of miles.

The transmitter is equipped to marry the electrical current from the control room with the high-frequency oscillations of the radio waves. In this process the audio signals from the studio microphone modulate (or vary the shape) of the radio carrier. It is rather like sealing a letter in an envelope—the audio signal being the letter while the radio carrier is the envelope. The transmitter engineers have to be constantly on their guard to protect the shape of the envelope by controlling the level or intensity of the audio modulating signal otherwise the sound quality becomes distorted and the transmitting equipment can be damaged.

Radio waves travel at the speed of light, that is 300 million metres per second (about 186,000 miles). The wavelength of a station is arrived at by dividing the speed of propagation by the frequency of the transmitter. It is usual to state frequency in kilocycles and so reduce the propagation speed to 300,000.[1] If we divide 300,000 m by 4,900 kHz (this is the same as dividing 300,000,000 by 4,900,000 Hz) we arrive at the approximate figure of 61 m —thus the announcer says: 'We are broadcasting at a frequency of 4,900 kilo-Hertz in the 61-metre band.' With a known frequency it is always possible to calculate wavelength and vice versa.

When you tune in a radio signal you are adjusting the aerial system to resonate in sympathy with the frequency of the selected transmitter. The circuit of your receiver then extracts the audio message from the envelope of the radio carrier and amplifies it to drive the loudspeaker thus producing acoustic pressure waves theoretically identical with those produced in the studio.

The sequence of steps from microphone to receiver is spoken of as the broadcast chain. A comparatively detailed knowledge of the studio and control-room elements of this chain is essential for technical operators and is also of great advantage to producers. These subjects are treated in the next two chapters.

Metre bands—their uses

The radio frequencies used for broadcasting are only a part of the whole electromagnetic spectrum which embraces radio and electric waves, heat, light and X-rays, and has wavelengths varying from over a mile in length to one millionth of a millionth of an inch. The radio broadcasting frequencies are divided into metre bands and each band has its own particular use.

1. The formula is: $\text{Wavelength in metres} = \dfrac{300,000}{\text{Frequency in kHz}}.$

Purpose	Band name	Frequency	Wavelength
Medium-range domestic broadcasting	Medium wave	525–1,605 kHz	571–187 m
Medium-range tropical broadcasting	Tropical broadcast band	2.3–5.06 mHz	120–60 m
World-wide long-range broadcasting	Short wave	3.9–26.1 mHz	75–11 m

In Europe and northern Asia the long-wave band at frequencies of 150 to 285 kHz is also in use. It is not practical in tropical zones.

There are also very-high frequencies (VHF) and ultra-high frequencies (UHF) of transmission used for television, high-quality frequency-modulated (FM) sound broadcasting and communication purposes. FM sound broadcasting covers only very limited local areas.

As the table above illustrates the different frequencies have different uses. The characteristic of propagation of a station—that is the way its radio waves are distributed—has a bearing on its coverage or the land area and the listeners that it serves.

A note on propagation

The radio carrier wave travels by two paths between the transmitter and the receiver. One path, that of the ground wave, is direct, while the other, known as the sky wave, is indirect. The sky wave bounces off an envelope of ionized gases, called the ionosphere, which surrounds the earth at a height of between 30 and 350 miles above our heads.

The height of the ionosphere fluctuates throughout the hours of day and night due to the action of sunlight on the gases. During the day and particularly at high noon the ionosphere absorbs some of the radio energy in the medium-wave band, in consequence of which listeners receive only the short-distance direct ground wave. Listening at any great distance from the transmitter becomes difficult.

At night the reflecting layers of the ionosphere rise and we receive both the direct ground wave over greater distances and also the indirect sky wave. The listening area increases. Sometimes however the two waves reach us out of phase and tend to cancel one another out causing fading of the signal. You should discuss the term 'phase' with your instructor or an engineer.

It is useful to know the propagation characteristics of your station as an aid in programming. It tells you where the signal is strongest and where it is weakest, and what the listener is likely to receive and not receive. It can help you to decide upon the most suitable programme technique to use for listeners in difficult reception areas. As a programme broadcaster it is your job to get the message through, but to do this you need to work within the technical realities of radio broadcasting.

Technical operations

In the studio the producer has the assistance of a technical operator, variously known as a studio manager, an audio engineer, control operator, panel operator or programme operator. He is a person of some importance as he acts as a go-between between the producer's programme intentions and the technicalities of broadcasting as understood by the engineer.

The duties of a technical operator vary but in general then can be summarized as follows:

1. To connect and balance microphones, and to adjust the volume of the recorded sound.
2. To switch on and operate all control room equipment such as mixing-panels, equalizers, turntables and tape recorders.
3. To set and monitor programme intensity levels.
4. To act as technical liaison officer between the programme producer and the engineer.
5. To make sound effects as required.
6. To complete and transmit musical copyright control forms.
7. To keep unauthorized persons out of the studio and control room areas.

The technical operator has a highly responsible job for he is the arbiter of the sound quality of the programme. In this he works closely with the producer, who should know the technical work as well as the operator does, but in the event of a dispute as to the technical suitability of the programme the final decision can only be made by the operator. He is the guardian of technical quality and must always maintain it at the highest standard.

Action projects

1. Find out all you can about the technical coverage of your station and plot the results on a map. What areas does it serve and what is its signal strength in these areas by day and by night? What do you know about the people living in those areas—their languages, religions, their work, their social needs?
2. List the frequencies and wavelengths used at different times of the day by your station or stations.
3. Visit your transmitter and collect material which can later be used in a talks or documentary exercise.

5   Getting to know the studio

The studio-suite, that is the studio and its associated control centre, is the workshop of broadcasting. A thorough knowledge of its characteristics and facilities is essential for any radio producer.

Studio systems

The group of studios in a broadcasting centre is known as the studio complex. In a simple centre it may consist of only one studio and a control booth. In a large broadcasting centre it will have several studios of different sizes, recording rooms, an echo chamber, a master control and switching room, and a quality control room. The various units of the complex are interconnected and can be joined together in a variety of combinations—more than one studio may, for instance, be used in a single production where isolation of the different sound elements is needed.

There are two principal systems of operational control.

In the continuity system all programme material, whether from another studio, or from tape, or from an outside broadcast point passes through a studio where an announcer and a technical operator are on continuous duty. In this system the announcer's continuity studio has final control of all programme material before it leaves the broadcasting centre for the transmitter. The announcer can break in upon or interrupt a programme at any time. He keeps a log of all material broadcast and comments on timing, suitability of content, sound quality, faults and other relevant matters. In effect he acts as over-all producer of the total programme output and is responsible for maintaining the broadcast schedule. The technical operator in the control position of the continuity suite selects contributing studios, pre-tests them and maintains final level control.

In the master switching system the continuity function is separated from announcing. It is divided between a senior programme officer, often known as the programme or studio supervisor, and an engineer. The supervisor is concerned solely with quality control and programme management. His engineering counterpart pre-tests contributing studios and pre-selects them for connexion to the transmission lines.

Studios in general

There are several different types of studios in the larger broadcasting centres and each is designed and intended for a different purpose.

The announcing studio is of small size and is equipped with a bank of turn-tables and suitable for announcing, news-reading, talks and record programmes.

The general purpose studio is furnished with a round table and chairs suitable for talks, discussions and is sometimes used as a dubbing suite for assembling documentaries.

The drama studio is specially constructed to re-create different acoustic environments and contains manual sound effects equipment.

The music studio is of considerable size and with a principal dimension of at least 12 metres.

The auditorium is built like a theatrette with raised stage and fixed seating for audience participation programmes.

All studios are built according to certain acoustic principles to provide quiet places where different kinds of performances can take place undisturbed.

They are constructed free of the structural walls of the buildings containing them so that outside sounds—footsteps in passage ways, traffic rumble, the clatter of office typewriters, sounds from the control booth loudspeaker—will not penetrate. They are generally rectangular in shape; ceiling height, width and length being calculated to give the best quality of sound. The materials used in the construction of the internal walls have special acoustic properties to absorb and reflect sounds at different frequencies.

The study of the behaviour of sound is known as acoustics and some knowledge of it is necessary for any producer as it determines his choice of studio and microphones and his placement of artists in the studio.

Sound

The audio spectrum. In the previous chapter reference was made to vibration as the source of all sound. The rate of vibration was described as frequency—that is a count of the number of times per second that the source moves backwards and forwards about its position of rest. Fast vibrations make high-pitched sounds and slow vibrations make low-pitched sounds. The extent of the swing about the position of rest—called the amplitude of the swing—determines the loudness of the sound.

We hear as a result of the pressure waves set up in the air by vibrating objects. These pressure waves impinge upon our ear-drums causing them to vibrate at the same frequency as the source and with proportionate amplitude. But for our ears to detect these pressure changes they have to be within a certain range of frequencies and have sufficient intensity.

The range of frequencies heard by human beings is known as the audio spectrum and it embraces all the frequencies between about 20 and 20,000 Hz. The actual range of the spectrum, however, varies from one person to another.

Usually only young people hear sufficiently well over the entire spectrum, particularly at its upper limit. Some animals, bats and dogs amongst them, hear sounds which are inaudible to human beings.

To get some idea of the audio spectrum ask an engineer to demonstrate it with a piece of equipment called an audio signal generator. You can compare sounds made by it at certain frequencies with musical notes on the piano: middle C on a properly tuned piano vibrates at 261.63 Hz.

Harmonics. The sound made by an audio signal generator will sound in tune with but not exactly alike its equivalent musical note. This is because a signal generator produces a pure note whereas natural sounds from a piano or a singing voice or any other instrument are seldom pure. Natural sounds contain harmonics.

A harmonic is a simple multiple of a fundamental frequency. The first harmonic of a fundamental of 1,000 Hz is 2,000 Hz, the second harmonic is 3,000 Hz and so on. Harmonics are made by sympathetic vibrations. In the case of the piano these are set up by the vibration of other strings and the frame and the woodwork. Harmonics in human voices occur because of sympathetic vibrations of the air in our mouths and nasal passages.

The proportional intensity of harmonics to fundamentals gives a musical instrument or a human voice its particular characteristic. This is why in listening to music or to people speaking we are able to identify the instrument or the person.

In the construction of a well–designed studio, materials are used in such a way as to maintain the truthful relationship of harmonics to the fundamentals. If the wall panels of a studio vibrate at the harmonics of certain frequencies they make the music or speaking voice sound unnatural. This is where knowledge of acoustics and a good ear for sound are important to a producer in his choice of studio.

Resonance. The sympathetic vibrations which occur in most materials at both the fundamentals and harmonics are called resonance. Loosely held studio panelling can become particularly resonant and can 'colour' the sound of a particular studio. Loose objects such as music stands, the clasps on musical instrument cases will all resonate at certain frequencies and it is often advisable therefore to remove these from the studio during a musical performance.

The body of air in the studio will itself resonate at certain frequencies. These frequencies are determined by the distances between parallel walls, the floor and the ceiling. The sum total of the room resonances of a studio is known as the eigentone of the studio and it gives each studio its own characteristic.

Reverberation time. Another factor which helps to give a studio its particular character is the reverberation time—that is the length of time which it takes for the body of air in a studio to come to rest once it has been excited by a sound. In technical terms it is the time taken for the intensity to fall by 60 dB (decibels).

The reverberation times of studios vary according to the purpose for which they are designed. In a good announcing or talks studio the reverberation time is generally between a quarter and a half of a second. A short reverberation time makes a studio sound 'dead'. A music studio needs to be 'live' and the accepted reverberation time is usually about two-and-a-half seconds.

In a well chosen drama studio the eigentones and reverberation times are likely to differ at opposite ends of the studio. One end is likely to be very brilliant or live while the other is likely to be dead. Curtains can be used to help bring about the change, to create different atmospheres in which through sound the illusion can be given of being indoors or out-of-doors. Where there are no such acoustical facilities the variation of environment can be produced by placing microphones close to walls or in corners.

It is a very good idea to spend quiet minutes in any studio listening keenly to judge its acoustics. Changes in the character of sound in dramatic and documentary feature programmes add interest for the listener.

Characteristics of the octaves. An octave is an interval covered by eight notes of a musical scale, the beginning and the end of the scale having a frequency ratio of 2 : 1.

The doubling of a frequency therefore raises a musical note by one octave, and conversely an octave rise represents a doubling of frequency.

For all practical purposes radio is concerned with ten octaves only. It is useful in music production and in studios having equalizing equipment to know something of the characteristics of the various octaves.

Octave	Frequency in Hz	Notes
1st	16–32	The low frequencies contained in musical bass
2nd	32–64	and rhythm section. Accentuation of 2nd
3rd	64–128	and 3rd reproduces piano music naturally
4th	128–256	but over-accentuation makes the tone rever-
5th	256–512	berant and offensive to music lovers.
6th	512–1 024	The middle and upper middle frequencies.
7th	1 024–2 048	Accentuation of the 6th and 7th gives a
8th	2 048–4 096	speaking voice a telephone quality and any
		length of listening leads to listener fatigue.
9th	4 096–8 192	The high frequencies. Accentuation of the 8th
10th	8 192–16 384	and 9th gives presence and makes a speaking
		voice sound as though it is in the room. The
		10th contains the tinkling of bells and musi-
		cal action noises.

Its directional properties. Sound travels in all directions outward from its source as a spherical wave. When the spherical wave-front becomes large it takes on the characteristics of a plane wave. The energy of a plane wave is concentrated in one direction, it is therefore directional. Whether or not a wave-front is spherical or plane at a given point from the source has to do with the size of the source in relation to the length of the wave it is producing.

For practical purposes it is sufficient to know that low-frequency sounds in studios generally retain their spherical nature whereas high-frequency sounds rapidly become plane waves. To make this into a useful statement we can say that low-frequency sounds tend to be non-directional while high-frequency sounds tend to be directional.

This phenomenon accounts for the difficulty experienced by music producers in getting sufficient 'power' out of a double bass in a jazz or high life band and the consequent need for closer microphone placement. The intensity of these instruments can be increased by placing them in the corner of the studio where the walls and floor begin to act as supplementary radiators.

The directional nature of higher frequency sounds needs to be noted in radio speech work, too. These directional sounds contribute to the clarity of a voice, hence the need to face a microphone when speaking.

Obstacles and reflection. When a sound wave strikes an object standing in its path it will be reflected by the object, the angle of reflection equalling the angle of incidence as with light. Where the object blocks the further passage of the sound an acoustic shadow occurs behind the object. The effect is known as the obstacle effect. It has a bearing on the use of studio screens and the placement of players at a microphone.

There is a strict relationship between the size of the obstacle and the length of the sound waves that it will block and reflect. It will only reflect or screen sounds having wavelengths shorter than the dimensions of the obstacle. Longer wavelength sounds will pass over the obstacle as though it was not there.

This fact limits the effectiveness of most studio screens in blocking low frequency sounds. These screens are seldom larger than 6 by 4 feet. They will therefore only block sounds of 6-foot wavelength and less. These sounds are those of approximately 190 Hz and upwards. Lower frequency sounds from drums or a double bass will pass over them.

Similarly a script held in front of a microphone by a speaker will screen the microphone from the higher frequency sound waves of 2,000 Hz upwards. Yet it is in this range that speech clarity belongs.

Wavelength. The wavelength for a sound of any frequency can be simply calculated. The formula is based upon the known fact of the speed with which sound travels through the air. This speed is 1,087 feet per second (331 metres per second) in air at 0° C; the speed increases approximately 2 feet per second for each degree centigrade rise in temperature. Sound also travels slightly faster in humid air than in dry air. For studio purposes the speed of sound is generally considered as 1,130 ft/s (344 m/s).

The formula for calculating wavelength is:

$$\text{Wavelength in feet} = \frac{1,130}{\text{Frequency in Hz}}.$$

Using the above simple formula we arrive at the following examples:

100 Hz = 11.3 foot wavelength,
1,000 Hz = 1.13 foot wavelength,
10,000 Hz = 0.113 foot wavelength.

With a rough knowledge of the relationship between frequency and wavelength it is possible to judge the likely effectiveness of studio screens and temporary screens which you can use when recording away from a studio, for example, in a hall or office.

The effect of temperature on the speed of sound should be taken into consideration when assembling musicians in a studio. If musicians keep their instruments out in the sun before entering a studio they will find it difficult to tune up quickly as the air in the instruments will be at a different temperature from the air in the studio. It is a sensible plan to bring instruments into the shade of the broadcasting centre, if not into the studio itself, some time before the broadcast or recording.

General. An understanding of the behaviour of sound in a studio is largely a matter of common sense, but common sense sometimes takes a little thinking about.

Get to know the characteristics of your studios by spending odd quiet moments in them and thinking about what you 'hear' in the silence. Regard sound as an invisible yet physical force. If you can understand it as a physical force you will be able to imagine how it can strike walls and be reflected by them and how it will set lightly held surfaces into vibration. By listening to a studio you may come to realize that the centre of any studio is a place where the turbulence of sound waves is likely to be at its greatest and that the centre is therefore a place to be avoided. You may also form the idea that sound sources are more likely to be naturally reproduced when they and the microphones receiving them are placed along the diagonals of a studio.

The studio is very much the province of a producer and the more he knows about it, the more confident he is in using it, the better his productions will be.

Microphones generally

A microphone is an instrument for measuring minute changes in air pressure. It converts acoustic energy into electrical energy and is therefore called an electro-acoustic transducer. It is a very delicate instrument and can be damaged easily by physical shock, i.e. by being knocked or dropped, and certain types of microphone can be damaged even by exposure to strong wind blasts.

The electrical force produced by a microphone is extremely small and must be protected against losses on its way through the cable from the microphone to the amplifier. The contacts made at wall connectors must be firm, the wires unfrayed and the shielding which protects the inner cables from stray electrical currents must be complete.

The heart of every microphone is a moving element of some kind. The nature of the element gives the microphone its particular characteristic and response. Some microphones are equally sensitive over the whole audio spectrum while others tend to discriminate against certain frequencies. Some have directional characteristics while others will pick up sounds coming from any direction.

It is important to know the characteristics and responses of the different microphones as this knowledge helps in the choice of the most suitable microphone for a particular purpose.

The diaphragm microphone

The diaphragm microphone was one of the earliest and is still one of those most frequently encountered in general broadcast use. Its moving element is a convex metal diaphragm, the smaller the diaphragm the better the response. The best and most expensive of this type of microphone is the electrostatic microphone. The most common studio diaphragm microphone is the moving coil, sometimes called a dynamic microphone.

The diaphragm microphone measures air-pressure changes much as does a barometer. It is very rugged and therefore much favoured for outside broadcasts and interview work as it can generally withstand reasonably rough treatment.

It does however have the disadvantage of being omni-directional or non-directional. It will pick up sounds coming from any direction even though its back is totally enclosed. However, because of factors having to do with the size of the diaphragm element, it is directional at high frequencies. It is, therefore, not generally favoured in studio work except for solo voice speaking when the speaker must address it directly within a distance of 6 to 8 inches. It is not really suitable for studio music recording, particularly in highly reverberant studios.

The ribbon microphone

The ribbon microphone has as its moving element a small corrugated ribbon of light metal. It has an excellent frequency response over the entire audio spectrum. It is extremely sensitive to shocks and vibrations through the floor and the microphone stand. It is sometimes called a velocity or pressure gradient microphone because it measures the velocity of sound between the forward facing and backward facing sides of the ribbon.

Because the ribbon is suspended in a plane about the axis of the pivot of the microphone the ribbon microphone is essentially bi-directional—that is to say it is sensitive only to sounds reaching it from the back or the front. It does not in theory pick up sounds coming from the sides. It is therefore an ideal microphone for studio use as it discriminates against sounds reflected from the studio walls.

It does have one disadvantage, however: if it is placed too close to the source of the sound, the microphone will tend to accentuate the low or bass frequencies. This means, in effect, that a speaking voice should be best addressed to a ribbon microphone from a distance of 18 inches to 2 feet. The tendency to accentuate the low frequencies is sometimes called bass end tip up. Some of the more expensive ribbon microphones have close working switches to overcome this effect.

A ribbon microphone is the preferred choice of most producers for dramatic work, studio interviews and music in the studio.

A hybrid microphone—the cardioid

The cardioid microphone—so named because the area of sensitivity is heart shaped—is a most useful uni-directional studio microphone. It discriminates against all sounds except those approaching it from the front.

The most common cardioid microphones either have split-ribbon elements which can be used out of phase to achieve the uni-directional effect or combine a ribbon with a diaphragm connected electrically out of phase. The split–ribbon cardioid has the better over-all frequency response.

The cardioid, particularly the split-ribbon type, is the most useful common microphone for music recording where, because of the nature of the studio, it is necessary to isolate the various instruments or groups of instruments in a band or orchestra. It is also useful in audience participation programmes where public address loudspeakers feed the audience area. Its non-sensitivity to sounds reaching it from the back reduces the incidence of feed-back—that is the howling set up in a circuit when sound chases itself like a dog chasing its tail.

Microphones in the studio

The choice of microphones for a production is the responsibility of the producer in consultation with his technical operator. A producer must therefore be very familiar with the sensitivity patterns and frequency responses of every available microphone.

It is also a very good idea when working on a multi-microphone production to plan on paper the placement of the microphones before entering the studio. This microphone plot can then be handed to the technical operator.

When two ribbon microphones are switched on at the same time a loss of bass response can sometimes occur. This is caused by one microphone being out of phase with another. It can be simply remedied by turning one

44

microphone around and listening carefully to the result until the bass response is restored.

Microphone balance

It is always necessary to establish the proper working distance between a speaker or performer and the microphone. This is called balancing. The object of balancing is to achieve a natural-sounding performance within the technical limitations of radio.

When two or more people are speaking at a microphone as in an interview or discussion they must appear to sound the same distance from the microphone although their actual distances may vary because of the varying strengths of their voices. The speakers must also be seated in the fully active response area of the microphone so that all the voices sound equally full and rich. If one speaker sounds off microphone or his voice is less clear, it is likely to distract the audience. This may call for the use of more than one microphone in a discussion.

Musical balancing demands a high degree of skill on the part of the producer and his technical operator. The first question is the choice of acoustic surroundings. A country singing party, for example, is usually heard out-of-doors in the open air. This is a dead acoustic and so the choice of studio and positioning within it must be arranged to have as little reverberation as possible. On the other hand a cathedral choir is usually heard in highly reverberant surroundings and these must be re-created in the studio perhaps by the use of a near and a distant microphone, or the addition of electronic echo. Another kind of acoustic is required for a high life band and still another for a small jazz group.

In musical performances a distinction is often made between a close and a distant balance.

In close balancing a microphone is placed close to almost every instrument and the output of the several microphones is mixed on the panel. It is not natural balancing but it is popular with jazz musicians and does much to make the performance aurally exciting. The distant balance, customarily used for studio choral groups, is arranged by carefully placing the parts of the choir or the various musical instruments at different distances from a single microphone. It gives a more natural but somewhat flatter effect.

A music producer needs to teach vocalists, particularly 'pop' vocalists, to work a microphone, that is to move slightly away from it for loud passages and closer to it for softer passages. This is true of some scenes in drama where a player may need to shout and must slightly back away from the microphone to do so.

Microphone perspective

Another important aspect of balancing in radio drama is the use of perspective effects to create the illusion of space and movement.

A dramatic scene in radio takes place—like a painting or drawing—in one plane. It is unreal. But the illusion of reality can be created by careful thought and skilled microphone placing.

This is achieved by having lines spoken and effects played at different distances from the microphone, and by having the actor move away from or closer to the microphone while speaking. When an actor moves away from a directional microphone while speaking his voice creates a spatial effect by exciting the studio resonances; an altogether different effect is produced if he moves to the side and speaks into the dead area.

In planning perspective effects it is important to remember that things which happen at the same time must happen in the same acoustic perspective. If two players at a microphone are supposed to be having tea together, their speech and the clatter of the cups must be in the same acoustic plane. If a friend calls to see them and knocks on the door, the sound of the knocking must be more distant. If one of the players then goes to open the door we must be made aware of his movement away; he can for instance talk to the other player while moving away; the door must then be opened off micro-phone, the new arrival greeted off microphone and then brought on to the microphone while talking. Ill-considered perspective effects can distract the listener and leave him dissatisfied with what he has heard.

Studio sound effects

Any producer regularly engaged in drama production or the production of dramatic scenes in documentaries and educational broadcasts should set about building a small collection of sound effects equipment. Sound effects equipment is not costly to acquire and can generally be built up from junk.

The use of sound effects is discussed more fully in the chapter concerned with drama, however some basic equipment requirements are listed here: a solid door on castors which can be wheeled about the studio (it need not be full-size provided it is sufficiently heavy; it can have a sliding window and a good selection of bolts, locks, buzzers and bells attached to it); a motor-car door mounted in a wooden frame or attached to a studio wall; a wooden framed walk-board; two trays, one containing sand and the other containing gravel; a paving stone or concrete slab; a bucket or tarpaulin splash tank; a dial telephone and ringer; a village-type mortar and pestle for yam pound-ing effects; a rain machine; odd items of crockery, cutlery, whistles, light switches, bicycle bells, wooden clap boards.

Sound effects are best allocated a separate microphone. The most suitable type is a moving-coil diaphragm because of its tendency to accentuate action noises. They should be closely balanced.

If a script contains many effects a special assistant should be engaged to produce them in the studio. They should be properly rehearsed before the acting cast arrives as it often takes considerable time to make a sound effect realistic.

Discipline in the studio

The producer of a radio programme has full responsibility for and must at all times maintain a proper discipline over his technical operator, contributors, actors and musicians.

The producer should set an example by his punctuality in the studio. He should see to it that microphones are set up according to his requirements and that the microphone cords will not obstruct movement. He should make certain that everything is in readiness for the performance.

Studio discipline is essential where a large number of musicians or actors are taking part in a production. The producer should be in control at all times; he should not tolerate unbecoming behaviour nor angry disputes. He must control his artists firmly to get the results he wants. He should not allow performers to leave the studio without his permission.

The authority to maintain discipline comes best from the man who is knowledgeable about his job and confident of his ability to do it.

Action projects

1. Enlist the co-operation of an engineer and have him demonstrate the frequencies of the audio spectrum using an audio signal generator. It is also useful to provide visual illustration of the relationship between frequency and wavelength on a cathode ray oscilloscope.
2. Make detailed studies of the studios in your broadcasting centre. Listen carefully to sound in each studio using voice, musical instruments and an audio generator.
3. Experiment with the directional properties of sound by using shrill whistles and sibilant voices. Notice the screening effect of human bodies in front of microphones.
4. Listen carefully to the output of different types of microphones and plot them on the studio floor using ribbon to outline the live and dead areas. Notice carefully how the high-frequency sensitivity drops off as a speaker moves away from the live axis.
5. Attempt to balance various types of performance beginning with a discussion having five contributors and work through to a large band.
6. Using the script in the Appendix, or a similarly suitable script, experiment with microphone perspective effects in a dramatic situation.

6   Getting to know
the production cubicle

The control centre of the studio-suite is variously named in different broadcasting organizations. It is sometimes called the control room, the production booth or the production cubicle. It is a sound-proofed room acoustically treated in a similar manner to the studio.

A full-scale production cubicle contains the following equipment: a mixing panel, a bank of gramophone turntables, two or more tape recorders and possibly a tape cartridge unit, talk-back facilities, a high quality monitoring loudspeaker, a studio signalling system, line and telephone systems connecting it with the master control room, shelving for tapes and gramophone records, an accurate clock with sweep second hand. An exceptionally well-equipped production cubicle may also have equalizing and echo equipment.

A producer must be thoroughly familiar with the facilities provided by this equipment and he should preferably be able to operate it.

Some production cubicles are designed and equipped so that one expert operator can manage all the equipment, thus affording a great degree of integrated control. In others two or more operators may be needed.

The mixing panel

The mixing panel, sometimes called the audio control desk, control console or dramatic control board, is the central feature of any studio cubicle. It may be a simple unit built by station engineers or a large professionally manufactured piece of equipment. Its basic functions are: to switch and mix various sound sources, to master control the over-all gain, to measure the gain.

The sound sources are studio microphones, gramophone turntables, tape play-backs, line inputs from other studios, lines from outside broadcast points, echo and equalizer lines.

The mixing panel makes it possible to blend music and music, sound effects and music, music and speech, sound effects and speech, speech and speech and to feed the total programme output to a tape recorder or a transmission line. The mixing controls are either rotary or sliding attenuators, familiarly called faders or pots (abbreviation for potentiometers).

Once the signals from the various sound sources have been mixed they pass as a combined signal to the master gain control, sometimes called the master fader, which is another attenuator.

Some control consoles have sub-masters. This is another attenuator which makes it possible to group fade a number of sources simultaneously, for example to fade a mix of two sound effects records and one music record behind a speaking voice by the use of one fader only—the sub-master.

Over-all control of the programme output is managed by the master gain control. This control is ordinarily set at the beginning of the programme and not touched until the final fade-out or unless a board fade is required. It is bad practice to control sudden rises in volume by use of the master fader; the particular source fader should be used when this occurs.

The over-all gain or volume intensity of the programme is measured by a meter. In most production mixing panels a volume unit meter—VU meter —is used for this measurement. The VU meter responds rapidly to sudden rises in gain, and drops almost as rapidly. By carefully watching the VU meter it is possible to anticipate rises. Another type of meter used in some panels is the peak programme meter—the PPM. The PPM is an accurate meter for measuring real peaks in amplitude of an audio signal; it clearly indicates averages and is in consequence much favoured by engineers, although its slow fall time is a disadvantage in production work.

Mixing and fades

Mixing of sound calls for a critical ear and a sharp eye on the VU meter. By mixing we can fade sounds in and out and blend them together in various proportions.

There are several kinds of fades and each has its established use in radio production. The term fade is generally applied to the fading in or out of a particular sound source.

The cross-fade or mix is the fading out of one sound while at the same time fading in another so that the two overlap for a few seconds. It may be used between two musical records or to blend an announcement with a record. In drama it is used to indicate a scene change: the roll of surf and the screech of sea-gulls cross-faded to the music of a night-club band would indicate a change of scene from the seashore to a night-club. Between one kind of music and another the cross-fade is generally quick, whereas in drama it can be slower.

The partial fade is used to place one sound against the background of another as, for instance, when an announcement is made over a record of music, or where a narrator tells the story of action taking place in the background. In a night-club scene we may first of all hear the band playing at reasonably full volume, this may then partially fade so that we can hear the conversation of two people in the foreground.

The term 'board fade' is used when all the sound from every source is faded in or out at the same time. A board fade-out may be used to indicate the end of something. It is followed by silence. Used in drama a board fade-out often indicates a change in time: the action of one scene board fades out into silence, and after two or three seconds of silence a new scene fades in. The board fade is like a cross-fade, but separated by silence.

The slow fade usually indicates passing of time in dramatic programmes. The length of the fade is a matter of artistic taste; generally the slow fade should never be less than 7 seconds and may last as many as 12. Slow fades must, of course, be really slow. They are sometimes used in music programmes for dignified or repetitive music. It is not good practice to fade out a music programme simply because the length of the music has been under-estimated.

The fast fade is used in music broadcasts to cut the length. It has to be very quick to be effective, and it is most important to make the cut at the end of a musical phrase. In drama, the fast fade is used to withdraw listeners rapidly from a scene. For instance, two players may be talking when one says: 'Let me tell you a secret. . . .' If we do not wish our listeners to hear the secret yet, we use a fast fade.

Another type of fade not made on the mixing panel is the self-fade; the actor in the studio fades himself by moving into or turning his head towards the dead area of a directional microphone as he is speaking. This is sometimes used also by a narrator in a studio documentary in introducing a scene.

All sound sources can be faded, but to be effective fades must be done with considerable skill. It is the producer's responsibility to determine the type and length of fades. This should be done during the preparation of the script and fading instructions should be clearly typed in capital letters on the script. During the course of the production the producer should warn his technical operator in the cubicle when a fade is coming and, at the right time, give instructions along the following lines, by way of example: 'Ready to fade seagulls . . . Fade . . . Mix to studio.' He should speak loud enough to be heard by the operator above the programme level.

Line levels

The very nature of broadcasting makes it necessary for minimum and maximum sound levels to be observed. If a signal is too weak it may be difficult to hear in the distant secondary coverage areas of the station. If it is too high the sound will be distorted and may in certain cases trip the overload devices at the transmitter and put the station temporarily off the air. The programme level has, therefore, to be strictly controlled. The problem facing the producer and his technical operator is to achieve the full programme intention within these lower and upper limits.

It is for this purpose that the mixing panel has a VU meter. The deflection of the indicating needle of the VU meter corresponds with the ability of the human ear to compare the relative loudness of successive sounds. The meter also indicates percentages of modulation and is sometimes made to read the real percentage modulation of the transmitter. It is therefore in every way a very useful instrument as it serves the producer by reading comparative sound levels and the engineer by reading the extent of modulation.

Every broadcasting and recording studio sets a figure representing the maximum modulation normally permitted. The exact figure on the VU meter varies from studio to studio and it is always important to find out this figure before using a studio. To assist in line-up of a studio's output around the maximum modulation pure tone is used—generally at a frequency of 1,000 Hz although some studios prefer 800 Hz or 400 Hz. Maximum modulation as set with tone by the master fader and read on the VU meter should never be exceeded for any sustained time.

To work within the lower limit of modulation it is sometimes necessary to 'cheat' a little. This is so in a drama where a whisper may be needed and in classical music which frequently has very low passages. The whisper and the low passage of music can be gradually raised in level without appearing unnatural as the human ear is not aware of level changes of two decibels or less. The likelihood of loss of signal strength at the lower limit of modulation should also be kept in mind when using the board fade as a time lapse device in drama—a 3-second silence on the cubicle loudspeaker may sound much longer to a distant listener.

Gramophones and the gramophone record

Music on gramophone records makes up a large part of the broadcasting day, and recorded mood music and sound effects feature prominently in much radio drama. The gramophone is therefore an important item of studio equipment and the record library of any station represents a large investment of programme money. Records and gramophones need to be treated with care.

The usual studio gramophone consists of the following: a low friction turntable driven by an electric motor through a belt or pulley system to rotate at 16, $33\frac{1}{3}$, 45 and 78 rpm (revolutions per minute), a pivoted tone-arm on a low-friction bearing, a pick-up cartridge with a gemstone stylus, an equalizer to adjust the frequency response playback curve to the record manufacturers' recording characteristics, headphones or miniature loudspeaker for cueing, a device for lowering the stylus gently on the record surface.

In some studios, particularly drama studios, a bank of three or four turntables may have a sub-mixer for mixing the outputs of several gramophones before feeding into the control console. Another device of great use in drama production is a facility for acoustic feeding—that is playing a sound effects record directly into a studio loudspeaker so that its output is picked up together with dialogue on the studio microphone. Many effects sound more realistic when fed acoustically.

The different record speeds have grown up over the years, the lower speeds becoming possible with the development of silent vinyl plastic surfaces. Mood music and sound effects are generally still recorded at 78 rpm as this speed is easier to handle and cue. Incidentally, do not overlook the possibility of playing 78 sound effects records at slower speeds to achieve unusual effects.

The playing stylus is very delicate and needs to be treated with great care as it is easily damaged. It is a small chip of gemstone at the end of a fragile cantilever arm. These gemstones are either synthetic sapphire or natural diamond. The life of the diamond stylus is about twenty times longer than that of the sapphire. A sapphire stylus needs to be changed after between 150 and 200 hours of playing.

The playing time of a record depends upon the playing speed, the number of grooves per inch and the size of the record. The standard 78 rpm disc has between 96 and 120 grooves per inch whereas the microgroove LP can have as many as 400 grooves per inch. The correct stylus—78 or microgroove—must always be used. A standard 78 stylus is about three times as large as the microgroove stylus and will therefore damage a microgroove record if it is used to play one.

Similarly great care should be taken in handling records, particularly microgroove records. The bottom radius of a microgroove is generally of the order of 0.0005 of an inch. It is highly susceptible to dust which can also lead to distorted playing. The disc should always be kept in its dust-jacket and never left unprotected on the cubicle floor or stacked against a wall. Particular care should also be taken with microgroove records when making a jump-cut—that is rapidly fading down, advancing the pick-up some distance and fading in again. A too-rapid lowering of the pick-up may pit the disc.

The gramophone library

Get to know your gramophone library very well and ask about the copyright regulations which your broadcasting organization recognizes.

Copyright regulations generally prohibit the re-recording on tape of gramophone records produced by the major manufacturers. However to assist radio producers in the use of music many specialist manufacturers produce libraries of special music which may be re-recorded provided a fee is paid.

The use of music in radio drama and the radio documentary can do much to create a mood or set a scene. However, much of the available music for this purpose is attuned to Western ideas. A good drama producer will try to find out what ideas this music conjures in the minds of his listeners and seek out indigenous music that can be used for similar purposes. It can be recorded in the studio and processed on a standard gramophone record.

The tape recorder

It would be hard to imagine modern broadcasting without the tape recorder yet the tape recorder is a comparative newcomer. It is today one of the most important items of studio equipment.

The principle of tape recording is comparatively easy to grasp. A ribbon of plastic tape coated with a magnetic material passes at a constant speed through the field of an electromagnet, called the head. An alternating current corresponding in frequency with the frequency of sound at the microphone flows in the head causing a series of magnets to be impressed on the tape. On playback the now magnetized tape again passes over a head inducing in it a flow of current. This current when amplified drives the loudspeaker which reproduces the original sound waves.

The mechanical part of a tape recorder is called the tape deck (sometimes the tape transport mechanism). The constant drive to the tape is provided by a capstan and pinch wheel. The tape deck also has two rotating platforms, one to hold the feed spool and the other to hold the take-up spool. It is important to understand that the drive is provided by the capstan and not the take-up spool.

A studio recording machine has three heads: an erase head to remove any previously recorded material, a recording head and a play-back head—in that order. A fine hairline gap separates the pole pieces of each electromagnetic head. The gap lies at an angle of 90° across the width of the tape. This gap must be kept clean otherwise the tape will be only partially recorded upon. The heads must also be regularly demagnetized, otherwise they fail to record and reproduce the upper frequency range—the range containing those precious frequencies which give clarity and presence to a recording.

The recording tape has a plastic backing of cellulose acetate, polyester or nylon. It is available in various thicknesses: the thicker and therefore stronger standard play or long play tapes are generally used in studios. Cellulose acetate tape is brittle and not suitable in the tropics. The thickness of the backing determines the length of tape on a reel of any given size. On this backing is deposited a fine coating of magnetic material. The coating must always face inwards towards the head and be in intimate contact with it. The plastic backing generally appears glossy to the eye.

There are two speeds used in most broadcasting studios—7.5 inches per second (ips) (19 cm/s) and 15 ips (38 cm/s). The lower speed is generally used for speech and field recordings, and the higher speed is used for music. There is a relationship between speed of tape and frequency response. In many recording studios speeds of 30 ips and 60 ips are used to obtain maximum quality.

Studio recordings are generally full-track, that is, they use the full width of the tape. Some portable recording equipment is half-track. A full-track recording can be played back on a half-track machine but it is not wise to play-back a half-track recording on a full track machine unless the second track has not been used, and even then it is not really advisable.

There are two equalizing standards used in tape recording, the American NAB and the European CCIR. Where equalization can be adjusted, it should be adjusted to correspond to the equalization characteristic of the original recording.

A word of caution about tape copying. It is not good practice to make copies at twice the normal speed although this does reduce the copying time. Special recorders are used for high-speed copying and these are so designed as to preserve the fidelity of the original recording. High-speed copying on ordinary machines causes distortion.

Tape handling

Tape should be handled with care. It is easily stretched and stretched tape will curl. A curled tape will not make proper contact with the tape heads.

Care should be taken to avoid the tape twisting when respooling. A badly twisted tape, even though untwisted, will cause drop-outs or slight loss of programme material.

The tape, like gramophone records, should not be handled with dirty or greasy hands. Small particles of iron filings can readily adhere to the coated surface of the tape and these may block the gaps of the tape heads.

It is not good practice to leave tape out of its containers as it will collect iron filings from the air. Nor should tape be left for any length of time in strong sunshine—for instance, on an office desk under a window. The rise in temperature brought about by the sun may impress a recorded signal on the tape so that it becomes difficult to erase it completely.

It is always safest to erase tape on a bulk-eraser before taking it into a studio or out on a field recording.

Tape editing

Tape is a very easy medium to edit. There are two types of editing: dubb-editing and cut-editing.

Dubb-editing means editing by copying the tape and leaving out or inserting additional passages. When dubb-editing make sure that the two machines to be used for it have recently been cleaned and demagnetized. Copying always leads to a rise in the background noise; this is less noticeable with a well-serviced machine.

Cut-editing is a physical process of cutting out unwanted passages and joining the tape together with a special pressure adhesive splicing tape. If ordinary adhesive tape is used for splicing the joints it is likely to become sticky after a short time, particularly in the tropics, and will ruin the whole tape. The cuts should be made at an angle of 60⁰ across the tape and the cutting done with non-magnetic scissors or a demagnetized razor blade. Joints can be made with certain types of tape by using a special solvent.

Good tape editing takes skill and practice. It calls for an attentive ear and an acute understanding of inflections in human speech. When editing material recorded in the field, pay attention to the background sounds. Joints between two passages, one with, say, a background of heavy traffic and the other without, are particularly noticeable and disturbing to the listener.

Echo

Echo or added reverberation has many uses in broadcasting. It may be needed for a scene in a drama, it may be used to heighten some effect in an announcement or in a documentary, and it may be used in modern 'pop' recordings as an effect.

Echo can be produced in several ways.

The studio complex may include a special echo room, a small room with highly reverberant wall surfaces and containing a loudspeaker and a microphone. The programme material to be echoed is fed from the control panel to the loudspeaker, picked up on the microphone and returned to the control panel. Sometimes temporary echo rooms can be rigged up at night in a broadcasting centre by using a stair-well or an entrance lobby.

Special echo units made of spring-steel wires or plates of sheet steel offer another technique for producing echo. The feed and return is similar to the echo-room method. There are also special tape echo units consisting of an endless belt of tape and several replay heads.

A useful and inexpensive way of producing echo is by studio tape-recorder. Since the recorder has both a recording and a play-back head, programme material can be recorded and played back at the same time. If the recorded signal is played back and then fed for a second time to the recording head the programme material will appear to echo. The amount of echo, or the ratio of echo to the original material, is controlled by the fader on the replay line. This tape-echo is more effective if the recorder is used at its highest speed.

Echo is a useful production device but like all novelties it should not be overdone.

The cubicle loudspeaker

The cubicle loudspeaker is generally a high-quality unit giving faithful reproduction of studio and recorded sounds. The best listening position is on the axis of the loudspeaker. The space between the loudspeaker and the producer and his technical operator should not be blocked by equipment, furniture or other persons.

The listening level should be high enough to allow comfortable listening but from time to time in the course of a production it is useful to listen at a lower level as this gives a better idea of how the programme may sound to listeners. Some control panels have a special dim switch which cuts the listening level by half.

An experienced technical operator will often find his ears to be as good a judge of programme levels as the VU meter.

Talk-back

All studios are provided with a talk-back device enabling the cubicle staff to talk to performers in the studio when the studio microphones are not switched on. But care should be exercised in the use of talk-back.

The talk-back level should be high enough for the studio artists to hear, but not so high as to deafen them.

When using talk-back speak clearly and slowly. There is no need to shout. Avoid the habit of using talk-back too often. If, in the course of a rehearsal, you find many points about which you wish to speak to your artists note them on your script and talk about them with your artists at the end of the rehearsal, do not constantly break in on the rehearsal through the talk-back. It can upset artists and you run the risk of not hearing some important part of the rehearsal.

Signalling

The simplest studio signalling system will generally have 'Stand by' and 'On air' signs. It may also have a cue-light device which can be flashed to warn artists. The cue-light can also be used to indicate a need for an increase or slowing down of pace.

But in addition to the use of light signalling it is useful to develop a code of hand signals. Hand signals can be passed very quickly through the glass separating the cubicle from the studio, and they can be much more expressive than simply flashing a cue-light. During the rehearsal the use of hand signals will pass messages quickly without need to interrupt the rehearsal by use of the talk-back.

The following are some commonly used hand signals:

To ask for level: Fingers of the hand bunched at the lips then gently spread out in the direction of the artist.

To move away from the microphone: Hand with palm facing artist pushed away fromlips.

To move closer to the microphone: Hand with palm held towards face brought closer to the lips.

To warn an artist to watch for cue: Point with index finger to your eye.

To indicate that you want a better balance when two artists are at the microphone: Weigh your right against your left hand like scales and then point to one of the artists and use the signal for move in or move away.

Stand by: The palm of the hand held upright above your head for all to see.

Go: The hand dropped and the index finger pointed clearly at the artist who is to start the programme.

Speed up: Extend the index finger and make a clockwise circle in the air.

Slow down: Draw your two hands slowly apart as though stretching a rubber band.

To indicate a fabe: Pat the air, palm down, and sweep it away.

There are many other hand signals you can invent to suit your own purposes.

When using any form of signalling be sure that it is understood by the artists. Inform them beforehand of any signals you are likely to make. When giving hand signals make them large and clear so that there is no danger of confusion.

Co-operating with engineers

Broadcasting is essentially team-work and engineers are very important members of the team. Get to know your engineers and the mysteries of their own master control room. You may find that the master control room contains many items of equipment of added use in programme work.

Every master control room contains some kind of equalizing equipment. This equipment is used to equalize—that is to build up or lower—the intensity of electrical currents at various frequencies. It can be used in radio programme production to simulate telephone effects in a drama by making a voice sound thin. It can also be used to clear up muddy recordings which you may have made on a portable tape recorder in poor acoustic surroundings or with a high level of low-frequency background noise. Some control mixing panels are equipped with equalizing equipment but, if not, you are sure to find it in the master control room, and it is a simple matter to interconnect lines from master control to the studio cubicle.

In return for the co-operation of the engineers give them your co-operation, too. If in the opinion of an engineer the technical quality of a programme is too poor for broadcast you can be sure he knows what he is talking about. It is your job to make the message of radio but it is his job to broadcast it.

Project

Check your knowledge of the technical facilities of production against the following list. Where your knowledge is short, arrange for a personal demonstration.

MICROPHONES

On our station we have the following types of microphones:

Type	Make	Pick-up pattern	Uses
....	....	....	....
....	....	....	....
....	....	....	....
....	....	....	....

MIXING PANEL

The mixing panel in use provides the following facilities:

Metering. What type of meter? ....
           What is the peak limit? ....
Inputs.   How many inputs? ....
           What are they? ....
           ....
           ....
           ....

Equalizing facilities?   Yes/No
Acoustic feeding for effects?   Yes/No
Can I operate it efficiently?   Yes/No

TURNTABLES

Can I operate them efficiently?   Yes/No
Are my fades smooth and good?   Yes/No
Can I put records on and take them off without touching the grooves with my
    fingers?   Yes/No

TAPE RECORDERS

What types of tape recorders are in use in our studios and for portable work? ......
....
Can I identify the various heads on each machine in use?   Yes/No
Do I know how to switch tape speeds and equalization?   Yes/No
Do I consider myself a good tape editor? How good?   Poor   Fair   Average
How long does it take me to locate, cut and splice a join? ....
Are my colleagues faster? Why? ....

Action project

With a portable tape recorder visit parts of your city or town and record local
sound effects not available in the library. Make several recordings at different
perspectives—some distant, some near.

Part III   Radio production

7   The radio producer

Someone is responsible for every programme that goes out on the air whether it is a simple record programme, a talk or discussion, the news, an outside broadcast, a musical performance or a drama. In the broadest sense the man or woman responsible for the programme who organizes it and brings it into the studio is a producer.

Yet the term 'producer' in radio is difficult to define. Perhaps we can best do so by briefly tracing the way in which the role of producer developed in radio broadcasting.

The early producers

In the early days of radio the stations had very small staffs. The most important man was the engineer who, more often than not, had built the broadcasting equipment himself; he also operated it and talked at the microphone. It was not long however before the engineer realized that he needed assistance and the work of making programmes was taken over by newly enlisted announcers.

At first the broadcast hours were very short—sometimes only 1 hour per week! But as attempts were made to popularize radio the transmission hours grew longer and announcers began to organize guest appearances of speakers, singers and musicians.

The announcer found himself cast in a new role. He had to coach the newcomers in the simple techniques of early broadcasting. He had to show his guests how to sit or stand at the microphone, how to avoid rustling paper and how to turn pages silently. He had to teach them all that he had learnt himself about broadcasting, how certain words were more readily understood than others and how spoken ideas were best assembled.

As this new aspect of the announcer's work began to grow in importance, some announcers gave up appearing at the microphone and became full-time organizers of programmes. They were usually well known in their own communities and took a lively interest in what people were thinking and doing.

While these early programme organizers were laying the ground plan of the profession, radio itself was changing. Better technical facilities came into use, audiences had grown considerably in size and they were more demanding. The scope of radio programming widened. Simple talks gave way to discussions, elaborate musical productions replaced many of the record programmes, radio drama began to make its appearance. More programme organizers were needed.

During a brief era specialists were recruited for this work—journalists, teachers, musicians and theatrical producers. However, few of them were able to make any great contribution to radio since they came from worlds far away from the studio and the microphone and had themselves to learn about broadcasting by trial and error. They had to rely heavily on the technical assistants, the 'production men' as they were often affectionately known.

The production man had grown up with radio almost from the beginning. He was at first an assistant to the engineer. He spent his life in studios and knew more about the programme use of the engineering marvels than did the engineer. His speciality was sound. He used it creatively to interpret in radio terms the programmes brought into the studio by the programme organizers.

The next step was inevitable. The production men—they were in fact the technical operators of their day—became producers. They employed their knowledge of sound to pioneer types of programme which were distinctively radio and not simply pale imitations of other kinds of performance and publication. They developed the first documentaries, newsreels, dramatized educational programmes and the poetic radio drama. The art of radio production was created by these men who made broadcasting a vital and exciting medium for the communication of ideas.

The producer today

The craft of radio production has been evolved in successive stages. The announcer who became a programme organizer and the production technical assistant who became a producer have both contributed something to the definition of a producer's work today.

From the announcer: an ability to express ideas in spoken words, a good command of language, a manner which puts studio guests at ease.

From the programme organizer: a lively interest in and identification with his community, a knowledge of available talent, some specialist interest, an ability to organize.

From the production man: a thorough understanding of the technical facilities, a keen appreciation of sound and inventiveness in its use.

The qualifications of a producer

The qualifications required of a producer, bearing in mind the development of the craft, may be summed up as follows.

62

The radio producer should have: a good grasp of the language in which he works so that he can edit scripts and advise speakers on correct pronunciation, a manner which wins the co-operation of artists, a skill in instructing and directing other people at the microphone, a good general knowledge and an interest in community affairs, a sense of responsibility, the ability to take the initiative and the enthusiasm to experiment, a creative turn of mind and a flair for showmanship, an ear for sound and the ability to conceive ideas in terms of sound, a thorough knowledge of the technical facilities and of the techniques of radio, a specialist interest.

The outline makes no reference to educational qualifications although some are implied. On this matter it is worth noting a Unesco recommendation regarding the recruitment of broadcasting personnel: 'Present standards are suitable but possession of certificates should not be mandatory. The emphases should be on talent, creative ability and an aptitude for broadcasting.'[1]

Action projects

1. The story of the development of the radio producer as outlined in this chapter has been a synthesis of his job as it developed in many parts of the world. To what extent does it differ from the development of the work of a producer on your station?
   (a) Seek interviews with several senior programme officers and find out how they began in broadcasting—as announcers, technical operators, engineers?
   (b) Who among the senior producers on your station do you most admire? What is it you like most about their productions? Listen carefully to their work and attempt to analyse it.
2. On this chapter a short statement was made about the qualities required of a producer. Using the following questionnaire can you measure yourself against it?

Questionnaire

1. How would you describe your grasp of the language in which you produce: Good? Better than average? Average? Poor?
2. Is your pronunciation always accurate? Are you aware when others mispronounce words? Do you feel you want to correct them? If you do correct them, how do they react—do they get angry, do they accept your correction?
3. Are you able to make other people feel at ease?
4. Do you consider that you have a sense of humour?
5. Are you a keen reader? How many newspapers and magazines do you

1. *Training for Radio and Television in Africa*, a survey by A. T. Quarmyne and F. Bebey (Unesco doc. COM/WS/64).

read in a week? How many books do you read in a month? Have you a good general knowledge of politics, science, sports and hobbies, literature, peoples' customs in other lands?

6. What kind of organizer are you? Good? Poor? Have you ever had artists fail to attend rehearsals? Why? Are you able to discipline artists and staff without losing their co-operation? When you go to the studio do you ever forget anything and have to return to your office—script, pencil, stop-watch, tapes, discs?

7. If you had to operate technical equipment which of the following could you operate with ease: turntables, tape recorders, the control console? What are the different patterns of a cardioid and an omni-directional microphone?

8. Do you have an interest in any special field of radio production—political broadcasts, music, sports, religious broadcasts, educational broadcasts, drama, news? Did you have this interest before entering broadcasting?

9. Do you consider yourself as having a good imagination? When you hear a programme can you imagine other ways of handling it and perhaps of making it more attractive or compelling?

8   The producer at work

The work of the producer can be broken down into the following four phases: assignment, preparation, rehearsal, performance.

The assignment

The assignment is the programme which the producer has been selected to make. A senior producer may be assigned a series of programmes for broadcast over a period of weeks or he may be assigned an occasional major production such as a monthly play or a fortnightly documentary. A more junior producer may be assigned short interviews or talks as contributions to a longer programme. Whatever the assignment it is necessary first of all to examine it carefully, making ourselves very sure of the answers to a number of questions.

What is the broadcast supposed to do—is it to entertain, to inform or to educate?

Who is the programme intended for—general listening or a particular section of the audience?

What is the most suitable way of handling the assignment—as a talk, an interview, a documentary or in some other way?

Without clear answers to these questions it is difficult to make much progress.

A programme of popular gramophone records intended for a wide general audience may fail if the compère is too talkative and spends too much time between records giving information of interest to him but which is of little interest to his audience. This may often happen with disc-jockey programmes where the audience may be interested only in the music as a background but has to suffer from a talkative disc-jockey filling time with irrelevant items of artist gossip. The producer must be clear in his mind as to which feature of the programme has the greatest audience appeal—the music or the talk.

Again, an educational programme can fail if the producer becomes too involved with entertaining scenes in the programme simply because he likes the dialogue or wants to display his virtuosity.

Unless the producer has his target audience clearly and constantly in mind he can very readily fail to satisfy his listeners. A programme aimed at a special section of the radio audience may need to be scheduled for broadcast at a particular hour—a programme intended for farmers, for instance, is unlikely to be heard by them if the broadcast takes place at a time when they are generally at work. Similarly the kind of approach the producer decides upon must be dictated by a knowledge of the target audience. For example, a medical talk intended for a general audience must obviously be written in popular terms so that everyone can understand it.

Careful examination of the assignment may reveal many hidden facets which may change our entire approach. An apparently straightforward talks assignment may, on closer examination, appear much more suited to documentary treatment perhaps because the scope of the subject is greater than we at first thought or because it may be easier to understand as a documentary than as a talk.

Unless we familiarize ourselves thoroughly with the assignment we cannot easily set about the next stage of preparation.

Preparation

Briefing. If the broadcast is to be written—as in a talk, a play or documentary —we have to select and brief the writer so that he clearly understands what is expected of him. Briefing is necessary, too, with many kinds of musical performances.

The briefing should include all we ourselves know about the assignment. It should suggest possible ways of handling the material. The best briefing is generally a long chat with the selected writer as this gives him an opportunity to discuss the subject and develop ideas. At the briefing session we can set down, too, the date on which we expect a first draft of the script—this date should be set well ahead of the broadcast to allow sufficient time for editing and re-writing should this later become necessary.

Bookings. Meantime, while the script is being written or the musical performance prepared, there are things to do in broadcasting house.

A tentative booking can be made for a suitable studio and recording channels, since in some broadcasting organizations there are not quite enough studios and the demand for them is heavy. The time needed should be carefully estimated and only this amount and no more booked. A 15-minute talk should not require more than a 45-minute studio booking; a 30-minute play may need two to three hours depending upon the expertise of the producer and the experience of his cast.

For certain major productions it may be necessary to book special facilities, for example an echo channel, or to arrange for the prior recording of certain material or special effects.

All bookings should be made well enough in advance so that the general studio-use plan can be dovetailed to cater for many producers. Similarly, notice of any necessary cancellations should also be given in advance so that other producers can take advantage of cancelled time.

At this stage publicity material should also be prepared for use by the announcer and for publication in radio magazines and newspapers.

Script editing. Once the script has been delivered it must be read carefully for conformity to the brief and suitability for broadcasting. This is the editing stage of the producers' work.

The writer may be asked to re-write it entirely or to re-write parts of it, or we may want to do this ourselves, with the author's permission, of course. If we hope to make the writer a regular contributor it is worth while to coach him in radio writing by showing him how some words are better for broadcasting than others and how certain phrases can be spoken more fluently than others.

A dramatic script needs special editing—sometimes called mechanizing —to prepare it for use in the studio by the technical operator and the actors. In mechanizing a script the control cues (for fades, mixes and such like) need to be written in and any special instructions to the actors.

Finally, the script has to be properly typed. It is useless to expect a good broadcast from a hand-written script even if it is a talk delivered by the author himself unless he is a very experienced broadcaster. A producer may find that he needs to train his typist in the proper layout of a radio script so that it is easy to read—sentences should not be broken between two typed pages nor, in dramatic scripts, should control instructions for the technical operator head a new page.

Casting. If we are handling a dramatic script, now is the time to cast it—that is, to select and book the actors who are to take part.

More about casting appears in the next chapter.

It is at this stage also that we select any mood music or recorded sound effects which are needed for the production.

Rehearsal

There are two distinct kinds of rehearsal: the dry-run, sometimes called a read-through, and the microphone rehearsal.

The dry-run is a rehearsal held in an office, a conference room or an unmanned studio—that is a studio without the equipment switched on. It reduces the pressure on studios and technical services. A straightforward talk may need only one dry-run whereas a complex drama may need several and the technical operator to attend at least one so that he can familiarize himself with the dramatic production.

As the name implies, the microphone rehearsal is held in a studio with all technical facilities working. Talks seldom need any microphone rehearsal if they have been read through before, but drama and documentary need several. Drama producers frequently rehearse parts of productions separately, with separate rehearsals for sound effects, music and actors before bringing all three elements together at the microphone.

The producer has much to do at a rehearsal; he has to ensure that the performance follows his interpretation of the drama—that the actors really live their roles, that the timing and pace of the performance are right, pronunciation correct, cues properly taken, that the performance is smooth and sounds as it should. Every producer finds his own way of handling artists to bring out the best in them. He needs to understand the temperament of the people he is producing—flattering or cajoling some, scolding others. He has to maintain discipline and assert his authority over the entire performance.

It is bad policy to interrupt rehearsals too frequently, for this breaks the continuity and sometimes makes artists very self-conscious. In early dry-runs interruptions are unavoidable but they are best avoided at microphone rehearsals. The producer should rather note corrections and then point them out to artists at the end of the rehearsal and, if necessary, re-rehearse those particular scenes again.

Eyes and ears need to work together at a microphone rehearsal but with the ears doing most of the work. The eyes need only follow the script casually and glance occasionally at the VU meter but the ears must concentrate on how the performance sounds. Small deviations from a written script are seldom important, whereas things which sound wrong are important—the listener hears the broadcast, he does not read the script.

Never be in a hurry at the end of a rehearsal. Use the talk-back to tell your artist or artists to relax and then go carefully through the script to discuss and explain the notations you have made during the rehearsal. Discuss the rehearsal also with the technical operator, as he may have noted important technical points to be passed on to the artists. Then, with the entire performance in your mind and all corrections and directions ready, go into the studio to give the artists their final briefing.

Rehearsal is the time to attend to the pace of a performance. Change of pace adds variety. In a musical production pace is varied by a proper arrangement of the numbers—a brief fast opening followed by a more gentle mood, then tempo again, sentiment and a lively finale. In drama the nature of the action itself sets the pace—romantic scenes call for slow and tender playing, violent scenes gain from rapid movement, scenes which point up the plot need to be played tellingly. A well-produced drama has a cadence and beauty of its own. The simple talk needs proper pacing, too—the opening should be slow so that the listener can become accustomed to the speaker, descriptive passages may be delivered rapidly but detailed argument needs to be deliberately spoken.

Preparation for the studio

Before attending the studio for a microphone rehearsal or performance the producer should make a last-minute check on his organization. Does he have sufficient copies of the script? Pencils? Records and tapes, if needed? Stop-watch? Only a badly organized producer arrives at the studio to find he must return to his office because something has been forgotten.

A check-list such as the one given at the end of this chapter is often useful.

Performance

The producer should arrive at the studio ahead of his artists and make sure that everything is ready—tables and chairs as required for a discussion, drinking water, pencils and note pads. How many microphones does he need? What kinds and where are they to be placed?

While his artists are arriving he can discuss some of the likely technical problems with his operator, but once his artists have arrived he must give his full attention to them. Artists should not be kept waiting too long, particularly if they are new-comers to broadcasting.

It has been said that once rehearsals are over the producer has nothing else to do but to sit back and listen. In a sense this is true—he does just listen. He listens to make sure the performance is as it was at the final rehearsal. He listens also to show his artists that he is listening.

For many artists the studio represents an unreal situation and so the producer must give them encouragement by appearing to be an interested and sympathetic listener. He must appear to be listening, not sitting with his head buried in his script or eating food or sharing a joke with his technical operator.

In a complex production the producer may have a good deal to do during the performance. There are cues to give to different artists, and he must advise his technical operator about coming tape, disc or studio cues. He must also keep an eye on over-all time, possibly indicating a speed-up here or a slow-down there.

Before releasing artists at the end of a performance check that the recording was satisfactory. Note on the production copy of the script the exact duration of the performance and the number of the tape. Then it is time to thank the artists for their performances—a small courtesy which pays dividends in goodwill.

Some guiding rules

This chapter has emphasized the importance of organization in the work of the producer, but much of this can be reduced to a few simple rules.

1. Make a full assessment of the assignment.
2. Select and brief the contributor; set deadlines for first draft and final script.

3. Book studios and other technical facilities.
4. Prepare publicity.
5. Edit script and cast the production.
6. Have the script properly typed.
7. Select mood music and sound effects.
8. Conduct dry-run.
9. Prepare to go to the studio.
10. Arrive at studio ahead of artists; advise technical operator of microphone requirements; supervise setting up of studio.
11. Microphone rehearsals.
12. Discuss rehearsals with the operator.
13. Give cast the final briefing.
14. Pay full attention to the performance.
15. Thank artists for their attendance.
16. Arrange payment of fees.

Action projects

1. Select three suitable subjects and assess them properly along the lines suggested in this chapter.
2. Write two types of publicity for the chosen subjects: (a) announcements to be spoken by the announcer; (b) short paragraphs for publication in a local newspaper.

A useful check-list

In some studios a check-list along the following lines has been found helpful. You may adapt it to your particular needs, and then sufficient copies made so that you have a supply handy for all your assignments.

The assignment:
Purpose of broadcast:
Target audience:
Method of handling (talk, interview, etc.):
Proposed date of broadcast:
Contributor:
Dates for first and second drafts:
Date for final script:
Facilities required: ,
Date and time of read–through:
Date and time of studio rehearsal:
Dates and times of effects rehearsals:
Budget allocated for assignment:
Checks:
1. Have I properly edited the script and written in all control instructions?
2. Have I instructed typist as to correct number of copies required?
3. Have I selected themes, bridge music, sound effects, tape inserts? Are tape inserts flagged?

4. Have I discussed studio and microphone plot with my technical operator?
5. Have I arranged note pads, pencils, drinking water for artists (in the case of a discussion or panel game)?
6. Am I completely familiar with the script?
   Have I marked cues and control instructions?
7. Have I sufficient copies of the script?
8. Have I forgotten anything?

9   Microphone talent

Good voices and friendly personalities at the microphone are the backbone of broadcasting. They catch the ear and hold our attention.

The producer may not ordinarily be consulted in the selection of staff announcers but he does choose all the other voices heard on the air—the voices which will be heard as the speakers in discussions, narrators in documentaries, compères in light entertainment and actors in plays. These voices fill the greater part of the spoken word air-time of any station; thus, the producer has a considerable influence upon the spoken word character of his station. It is essential that he be a good judge of microphone personality and be able to uncover it in the talent he engages.

What is microphone personality?

Microphone personality quite often bears no relation to a person's real character—it is a blend of voice quality and manner of delivery.

A good microphone personality calls for a well-placed voice and a relaxed and friendly manner. The best microphone voices are in the middle to low registers—neither so shrill as to be annoying nor so deep as to be unclear. Microphone personalities should sound confident and self-assured, not tense or hesitant; they should talk with us, not at us. The phrasing and the pacing of their speech is easy and natural, not forced nor jerky. Above all they sound sincere.

These are the qualities which attract us to a voice and they are the basic attributes of the best of the leading microphone personalities.

Many voices fill the air during the course of the broadcast day and something different is expected from each one of them but all must have a discernible microphone personality.

A producer should study the voices he hears on the air from his own and from other stations. He should try to analyse what he feels about each voice he hears—what he likes and dislikes about them. In this way he will sharpen his appreciation of the spoken voice and become more selective in his choice of microphone talent.

Speaking at the microphone

Speech is controlled and articulated breathing. Good breathing is therefore essential to good speaking.

A relaxed but erect position with elbows and forearms resting on the table makes breathing easier than a slumped position. The hands should be kept away from the face as a hand cupped under the chin will restrict movement of the jaw or held to the cheek will distort the facial muscles. The jaw, the facial muscles and the lips must all have free movement when speaking.

Simple breathing and articulation exercises are an aid to good speaking. One of the simplest breath-control exercises is to inhale and exhale while silently counting a range of numbers—say from one to four, and gradually extending the range with practice. The time taken to inhale should equal the time taken to exhale. Waggling the jaw from side to side for a few minutes each day helps the jaw movement. Expelling air through closed lips also helps to relax the face and strengthen control over lip shapes and so aids articulation.

Even the best speakers will from time to time stumble over a phrase. But the incidence of stumbling can be reduced by practising difficult tongue-twisters.

The microphone should be spoken to as one would speak to a friend sitting near by. The manner should be neither too intimate nor too remote. Many good microphone speakers have in mind a close friend when at the microphone.

Phrasing

Punctuation for speech differs from written punctuation. Written sentences are often long whereas spoken sentences are almost always short, or they appear to be short because of the phrasing.

The general rule in spoken phrasing is to speak sentences which can be carried on a single breath without forcing the breath, and speaking together ideas which are thought of together.

It is useful to mark radio copy—the script or news item—indicating natural breath pauses. If we marked the above two paragraphs for spoken speech, the script might look something like this:

Punctuation for speech / differs from written punctuation . . . written sentences are often long . . . whereas spoken sentences / are almost always short / or they appear to be short . . . because of the phrasing. The general rule in spoken phrasing / is to speak sentences which can be carried on a single breath / without forcing the breath . . . and speaking together / ideas which are thought of together.

The stroke (/) can be used to indicate short pauses, two strokes and more for longer pauses and dots (. . .) for still longer pauses.

In spoken language emphasis can be given to words and ideas in several ways. The most common way to emphasize a word is to speak it with slightly more force than the other words surrounding it—this is a kind of vocal underlining. But another way is to lengthen the word in speaking it. This gives the word added importance. The same principle can be applied to phrases: those to be emphasized can be spoken with slightly more force or they can be lengthened.

Variation in pace helps to make speech sound interesting. A talk given at the same pace throughout sounds dull and monotonous whereas the talk which changes in pace and rate is more likely to hold interest. In this regard speech is rather like music where change of tempo heightens interest.

The announcer and newsreader

Good speech is particularly important for the announcer and newsreader. The announcer is the anchor-man of a radio station. He may be heard only briefly but he is heard throughout long hours of the day and over a period of years he can exert considerable influence on the speech standards of listeners.

Great care should be given to the selection of announcers particularly where the *lingua franca* of a country may be a foreign language. The standard of speech observed by the announcer and newsreader should stand as a model for others to follow.

It is generally said of the announcer that he should have: clear diction, correct pronunciation in every language that he uses, the ability to read easily and fluently and without any distracting vocal mannerisms or regional accents, an ability to communicate ideas clearly, a pleasing, friendly and acceptable microphone personality.

An announcer must necessarily be well informed over a wide range of subjects—music, sports, current affairs. The announcer who is also a newsreader must keep up to date with the background to the news and thoroughly familiarize himself with the names of people and places which appear in the news.

A good pronouncing dictionary and a pronouncing gazetteer should be part of the professional library of an announcer. He should also listen to foreign news broadcasts in order to learn to pronounce the names of new political figures as soon as they appear in the news.

The narrator

The narrator features prominently in many different kinds of broadcasts—the documentary, the educational series and the magazine programme.

Narration differs from newsreading. The newsreader is more formal and deliberate in his delivery whereas the narrator is often a more friendly and colloquial character. He is called upon to be much more descriptive in his delivery than is ever expected of an announcer. His pronunciation must be as faultless and his grasp of language equally as good as the announcer's.

Actors, being accustomed to an emotional style of delivery, often make

74

the best narrators but if none are available it is worth searching the ranks of lawyers and clergymen.

Other compères

There are many different kinds of compères in radio and it does not always follow that the man or woman who is a master in one field is necessarily as good in another.

The personality compère is the host to a light entertainment programme. He is generally the kind of person who appears to be everybody's friend. He needs an outgiving quality in his personality and a keen interest in other people. He is essentially a master-of-ceremonies and should not feel self-conscious on a public platform.

The sports commentator needs to have a keen interest in and a good knowledge of the particular sport he compères. Quick eyes and a ready ability to describe what he sees are essential to his make-up. He needs to express excitement in his voice without raising it to fever pitch.

The adjudicator-compère is the linchpin of the discussion programme or panel game. He introduces the subject and speakers, keeps the discussion moving and summarizes the points of view expressed. He needs to have a quick mind and a ready ability to assemble facts.

Finding talent

We noted two chapters earlier that a producer must have a lively interest in his own community. This is at no stage more obvious than when it comes to discovering and recruiting microphone talent.

Radio broadcasting is a community activity and the popular station is generally the one which is closely related to the community it serves.

A radio producer should always be in touch with his community and should attend all manner of public performances, lectures, theatres and university debating societies as the places most likely to produce new talent. The radio producer who sticks close to broadcasting headquarters tends to become more and more remote both from his audience and the talent pool.

It is good practice to keep a talent register, the exact nature of the register depending upon the particular field in which the producer works. Some producers are interested in finding good speakers to give talks or participate in panel discussions; others are interested in narrators and actors. All producers who engage outside talent need to keep a register of this kind.

A typical entry will contain information about, say, a speaker, the subjects he can talk about or discuss, his address and availability, a note on his microphone personality and the dates on which he has appeared and the fees which have been paid to him.

Actors and drama auditions

One of the problems facing drama producers in countries where there is little theatre activity is to find actors for the radio. Since there is insufficient work to ensure a professional actor a living, the drama producer must rely upon amateur talent, usually to be found among the various kinds of little theatre groups.

He should regularly attend play readings and performances organized by little theatre societies and university dramatic clubs, and invite those he selects to attend a studio audition.

Auditions

Auditions should be properly organized and held once every two or three months. About eight people—certainly a maximum of ten—should be invited to attend. The organizing producer should seek the co-operation of other producers in forming with him an auditioning panel so that an average can be taken of the impressions of several listeners.

The auditionees should be invited to bring material of their own, although audition scripts, either short scenes from dramas or specially written scenes, should also be available. These scripts should give the actor an opportunity to show his ability in different roles—romantic, formal, tragic and so on.

The studio should be curtained off from the control cubicle for auditions so that judgements will be based on sound rather than on appearance. The auditioners should note their impressions on a report sheet (an example is given as Appendix 1 to this manual). The form of reporting should be such as to permit the auditioner to note immediately his first impression about the type of character suggested by the auditionee's voice.

People's voices differ and we are all inclined to gain an impression of a person from his speaking voice. The impression needs to be immediate and strong in radio drama if we are to avoid mistakes in casting.

Casting errors in radio make nonsense of what might otherwise have been a good play. There is nothing quite as absurd as a woman with a mature and rounded voice heard in the character of a teen-age girl or a softly spoken and light-voiced man playing the part of someone in authority. The voice must suit the character.

The audition has this dual purpose—to separate usable from unusable microphone talent and to build up a talent register of characters.

We first concern ourselves with age—what age does the voice suggest? A young person or an old? How young, how old? Does it suggest a romantic person or a motherly or fatherly person? Does it suggest someone who is meek, or does it suggest someone in authority who is used to giving orders and having them obeyed?

Having established these character traits we can then go on to assess the voice in terms of personality, acting ability and whatever else interests us. An actor, since he has to play fictional characters, does not need to have the ideal microphone personality.

Once we have heard an auditionee at work—generally in two or three scenes totalling perhaps 15 minutes of playing—we can grade his ability. Many studios grade auditionees in the following four categories:

A. Immediately useful. Can employ at any time without fear of bad performance.
B. Performance patchy but auditionee obviously has ability which the producer can develop. Use in small roles.
C. Rough performance but some acting ability. Needs more experience but not at the producer's expense. Could use in minor roles in an emergency.
D. Unsuitable. Do not encourage to return.

Where an auditionee falls into either of the first two categories in the opinion of all members of the auditioning panel a cast card can then be made out for him. Below is a type of cast card which is useful.

Name:	Sex:
Address:	
Phone:	Voice age:
Languages:	
Accents:	
Can double:	
Voice quality:	
Available hours:	
General notes:	

The section for general notes should carry an impression of the ability of the auditionee to take direction. Some actors can very rapidly pick up what the producer means where others have difficulty in doing so. Information of this kind is also of help in casting.

The reverse of the cast card can be used for notes about the parts the artist has played, the dates and names of the productions and the fees paid.

Often actors who fall into category C can be developed successfully as narrators. Some producers believe that a 'failed' actor makes the best narrator.

Standards in speech

Every broadcasting organization sets a standard in speech, the standard aimed at by the station's announcers. Other speech work handled by producers should not fall below the set standard.

A producer must equip himself to correct the pronunciation of his artists at any time. The general standard of spoken language broadcast by any station is an important aspect of the general educational role of broadcasting.

Action projects

1. Analyse the microphone personalities of three broadcasters whom you find impressive. List the qualities which make them appear to you to be outstanding.
2. Using the audition report sheet at the end of the manual try to discover what impressions of character you gain from a group of auditionees.
3. How successful are you with the following tongue-twisters: I chased a big black pug pup up Upper Parliament Street. Essau Wood sawed wood and all the wood Essau saw Essau Wood would saw. Latticed leatherette looking like llamas leather.
4. Try reading aloud a descriptive passage of poetry, record it and have your friends or associates criticize it.

Radio writing

Very little broadcast material reaches the air without first having been written down. This is because of the technical nature of radio production, the strict time limits observed by most stations and the fact that good extemporaneous speaking at the microphone is a rare skill. For some kinds of broadcasting, such as the documentary and drama, a script is almost always essential.

The producer is concerned with radio script, sometimes as the author and always as the editor of a broadcast.

How radio writing differs

Radio writing differs from writing for publication imprint because the medium is different. Broadcasting is a form of living publication, it is not static but something which moves forward in present time. This calls for a different approach—a difference in style.

The reader of a newspaper or a magazine can select or reject paragraphs or whole stories as the fancy takes him. When he is not clear in his understanding of the author's meaning he can always re-read. This is not so of radio. The listener has to take everything as it comes or not listen at all. When he is unclear he has no means of referring back to clarify a point. A radio-script writer must therefore seek to hold the listener's rapt attention and go to considerable pains to ensure that the mean ing is clear and understandable at every stage of a talk or story as it progresses.

Another distinctive characteristic of radio writing is that things heard on the radio appear to the listener to be happening now. A broadcast is not a report of something past and gone—even the act of newsreading is something taking place at the same time as it is heard.

Above all radio writing is writing for the spoken word and everyday speech should be the guide to the words we use and the manner in which we use them. In talking with one another we use familiar words. We assemble what we have to say in short phrases and seldom put our ideas together in the kind of lengthy paragraphs which we may write. We put forward our ideas directly, not cluttered with small details nor involved in rambling parenthesis.

From these characteristics of radio writing we may deduce a series of rules.

Some rules

Use words which are in everyday use and are readily understood by the majority of people. This does not mean to say that we should use only simple words to the exclusion of all others. Where it is necessary to use an unfamiliar word it should be explained or enlarged upon in a short explanatory sentence or a short parenthesis.

Sentences should be kept short. But we must avoid a series of short staccato sentences which would make a speech sound jerky. Variety in sentence length makes a speech sound interesting. In general, however, the length should tend to be short rather than long. A sentence should never be longer than the number of words we can easily carry on a breath.

Avoid dependent clauses and clumsy inversions. Dependent clauses and inverted clauses are quite common in written matter but we seldom use them in normal speech. For example we may write: 'Longing for a cold drink, as he had walked many miles that day under a hot sun, Festus walked into the first bar he came to in the village.' In radio style the idea may be better expressed this way: 'Festus was thirsty. He had walked many miles that day and the sun had been agonizingly hot. He entered the first bar he came to in the village.'

Use descriptive words where possible but use them with care. The radio listener has only words to guide him and to sketch pictures which he would otherwise see with his eyes. The use of a descriptive word helps him to see the picture. In the example above 'agonizingly hot' says more than simply 'under a hot sun'. But descriptive words can be over-used if a script is filled with them. Descriptive words are better than figures where it is possible to use them— 'twenty minutes walk away' says more to the listener than 'a mile away'.

Speech has rhythm and speech rhythms should be kept in mind when writing radio script. A radio script should flow with the fluency of poetry. It helps to carry the listener along and it holds his attention.

Some of the best of radio dramas and radio documentaries have been written by poets who have a flair for the rhythms of language.

A radio script should display an element of 'nowness'. Whatever the broadcast, as far as the listener is concerned, it is happening now. It is an immediate and a personal experience. This should always be kept in mind when writing for radio. The choice of viewpoint from which a script is written, the choice of words, the author's approach and the enthusiasm with which he writes all have a bearing on the sense of immediacy.

Compare the following two examples. Which of the two styles has this sense of immediacy about it? Why?

'This new variety of corn has been developed especially for farmers in the drier zones. It is not subject to the types of crop disease which affected the older varieties.'

'If you're farming in the drier zones you'll be interested in this new variety of corn. It has been developed especially for you. You'll find that it doesn't suffer from the diseases you've known with the older varieties.'

Re-statement helps the listener to get the message. In radio broadcasting the listener must get the message immediately and clearly. We can help him to do this by re-stating in another way what we have already told him. A simple example: 'Water for children should be boiled. It should be heated over the fire until it is bubbling and steaming.'

By following these simple rules all radio writing can be made more effective. They apply equally to all kinds of radio scripts.

Narration and dialogue

Narrative and dialogue are the two ways we have to tell a story, whether it is a story of fact or a story of imagination. The narrative is a monologue—one person talking—while dialogue involves two people or more.

The narrative is a much used device in radio. In the opinion of some writers the narrative is radio's highest art form. The narrative may be the simple linking speeches in a magazine programme or it may sustain a whole drama. Good narration can be compared with oratory although the style is more personal and intimate. At its best it is a form of heightened prose and has about it an element of drama. At its worst it is a stodgy mass of words used because the writer has run out of better ideas for handling his subject.

Narrative should be used sparingly if it is to be effective. Too much narrative, uninterrupted by action or other sounds and voices, makes a documentary sound dull. If it is over-used in drama it holds up the action of the play.

In dialogue a story is told through the conversation of people. It must tell us all we need to know—something about the characters and personalities of the people of the dialogue, what they are doing and where they are. It is very like everyday speech but with the irrelevances removed. Dialogue writing is never speech making—we don't make speeches to one another in everyday conversation. The lines given to the actors to speak are generally short and the speeches are frequently interrupted by other actors in the play.

Compare the following:

OLU: I can't understand why you didn't speak to me yesterday. I was walking in the street as I always do in the afternoon when you came by on your bicycle. In the past you have always stopped to talk to me but yesterday you rode on as though I wasn't there.

FESTUS: I would have liked to have stopped to talk to you, Olu, but I was in a hurry because I was late for work. It was the second time I have been late this week and the boss told me that if I was late again I'd get the sack.

OLU: Oh, well, I understand but you could at least have waved to me.

The dialogue is stilted because the two characters each make speeches at one another rather than converse with one another.

OLU: What was wrong yesterday, Festus?

FESTUS: Yesterday?

OLU: Yes. I was walking on the street when you went by on your bicycle.

FESTUS: Oh, I was in a terrible hurry.

OLU: But you generally stop and talk to me—

FESTUS: Yes, I know. I'm sorry, Olu. I didn't mean to be rude. It was just that I was late for work. The boss said he'd sack me next time.

OLU: Oh, I'm sorry . . . but you could at least have waved to me.

FESTUS: Next time I will, Olu.

By breaking up the speeches the exchange of conversation sounds more natural.

Narration and dialogue both have their places in radio story-telling. Dramatic scenes involving dialogue can be used to good effect in some documentary and educational broadcasts; they can lighten the load on the narrator and help to hold interest in what may otherwise be dull passages. Similarly the narration can be used in drama to bridge scenes and to indicate the passage of time, although most radio dramatists try to avoid narration if it is possible to do so. Narration should never be used in drama as a substitute for action.

Mechanizing a radio script

A radio script must contain everything that happens—the words which the listener hears and the control instructions for the technical operator and the actors. The process of writing in the control instructions is in the province of the producer and it is sometimes called mechanizing. Some radio dramatists will do this work for the producer but where the dramatist does not then the producer must do them himself.

Mechanizing a script requires considerable thought and great attention to details. The guiding principle is this: if it is not in the script, it is not in the broadcast. The script as it goes to the studio must contain all that is to happen and indicate who is to do what and when.

For example a script as submitted by an author for a play may contain the following short scene.

YINKA: Yes, thank you, I will take a cup of tea. [*He pours it out, then starts choking and falls dead.*]

What is the actor supposed to do? Is he going to carry all the action himself? And if he does will it be clear to the listener? The author knows what he has in mind but the script in its present form is hardly suitable for the studio. In editing and mechanizing the script the producer may set out the scene in the following way.

1. YINKA: Yes, thank you, I will take a cup of tea.
2. [*Effects: Tea poured into cup on mike.*]
3. YINKA: It looks rather strong. [*He sips. Pause. Gasp.*] What have you done to me? [*He begins to choke.*]
4. [*Effects: Cup drops and smashes on floor.*]
5. YINKA: You . . . [*choking*] you . . . you've poisoned me! [*Long agonizing gasp for breath.*]
6. [*Effects: Sound of body falling to floor.*]

By mechanizing the author's original script we have put it into a form which can be acted out in the studio. The work has been divided between the actor at the microphone and an operator to make the effects of the pouring of tea, the cup dropping and the actor falling dead. All cues—that is everything that happens—have been numbered as this reduces rehearsal time by making back references easier. The producer can quickly say: 'We'll try cues 4, 5, and 6 again.'

In editing and mechanizing a script the producer may have to write some additional lines particularly where the author of the original script is not familiar enough with the techniques of radio.

As another example, a script as submitted may read:

MABEL: I thought you said George would be here.
DAVID: I did. He'll be here any minute. [*Knock on door; door opens; George enters.*]
DAVID: George!
GEORGE: Hello there!

If such a scene was played as written it would sound rather funny—as though George was waiting behind the door to hear his name. It is a technique sometimes used in light entertainment comedy but it is out of place in a play. The scene would need to be re-written as follows.

1. MABEL: I thought you said George would be here.
2. DAVID: I did. He'll be here any minute.
3. MABEL: I hope—
4. [*Effects: Knock on door off.*]
5. DAVID: That must be him now [*going slightly off mike*]. I'll open the door.
6. MABEL [*projecting off from on*]: Tell him he's late!
7. DAVID [*off. Mumbled*]: Yes, I will . . .
8. [*Effects: Door opens off.*]
9. DAVID [*off*]: Hello George, come on in.
10. GEORGE [*off*]: Sorry I'm late, David.
11. [*Effects: Door closes off.*]
12. GEORGE [*off but coming on*]: Is Mabel here yet?
13. DAVID [*coming on*]: Yes, she's waiting for you.
14. MABEL [*on*]: Hello George. You're late.
15. GEORGE [*on*]: Yes, I'm sorry Mabel, I got delayed.

By re-writing the scene we allow some time to pass for David to walk across to the door and open it and then return to where Mabel is seated or standing. We have written in additional lines, some to be spoken away from the microphone, to allow for the passing of time.

While mechanizing a dramatic script for the studio the producer can give thought to the questions of perspective which were raised in an earlier chapter when discussing microphones. In some scenes in drama, action will flow—or appear to the listener to flow—away from or back towards the microphone. While mechanizing a script the producer must always ask himself: Where is my microphone?

In the scene we have just read the microphone begins with David and Mabel and it remains with Mabel while David goes away to open the door for George. We could have staged this scene the other way round with the microphone apparently following David, but we would then have had to have given some lines to be spoken by Mabel from 'off mike' to indicate movement and to show that she was still there.

The terms generally used in a script to indicate perspective changes are:
Off and *slightly off*—these could be (*off back*) or *off* (*side*) depending upon the type of acoustic required. Off back from a directional microphone excites room resonance and gives the impression of space, whereas off to the side of a directional microphone means that the actor works into the dead area and the space effect is not created.
Projecting—which means that the actor pitches up his voice as though speaking to someone at a distance. It also creates the illusion of space.
Script mechanizing doesn't enter into talks work and only to a limited extent in programmes other than drama. In a straightforward documentary it may be restricted to music and tape insert cues. But where any kind of mechanization is called for it needs to be logically thought out from the viewpoint of how the action will sound and the instructions for the technical operators and actors need to be set out clearly in the script. By doing all this work in his office during the editing of the script the producer frees his mind to concentrate on the performance when he is in the studio.

How many words to a minute?

Speaking rates vary from one person to another, from one language to another and from one programme to another. News is generally read at a rate of 120 words per minute. The average rate in a dramatic programme may be as high as 160 words per minute.

In estimating the length of a script we must take into consideration the nature of the programme, the size of type and the length of each typed line. It is generally safe to assume that twenty typewritten lines equal 1 minute of reading time—that is 3 seconds a line. But until experience teaches otherwise the best way of timing a script is to read it through aloud.

A final word

Good writing is good writing in any medium. The established rules of composition apply as much to radio as they do to writing a letter, writing for a newspaper or writing a book, but in writing for radio we must remember that we are writing for the spoken word.

Many established radio writers chatter away to themselves as they write, savouring each phrase on the tongue to test its sound and judge how easy it is to say. It is a good principle to follow—if you cannot say it, if it does not sound natural and easy, then do not write it. And remember that a radio script is both a creative piece of work and a cue control sheet for the technical team engaged in the production.

Action projects

The following incident is written as a narrated story. Try to adapt it as a dialogue. The completed dialogue script should not run more than two and a half minutes.

'I discussed with the Desk Sergeant at the police station the question of my missing money. I clearly remember having had five pounds in notes in the house yesterday morning but it wasn't there today. I was very concerned at its loss as it was money I had set aside to buy my wife a birthday present.

'The Sergeant was offhand in his reaction, almost as though he resented my presence—as though I was adding to his work for the day. He may have thought I was making up the story. He asked me where I had kept the money and who would have had access to it—children, my houseboy, a casual visitor or perhaps even my wife.

'I told him I had left the money on a table in my bedroom—or at least I thought I had. The children wouldn't have found it as it was a strict rule in our house that they never entered my bedroom. It was unlikely that my wife would have taken it.

'He pressed me with questions. Was it on the table or in a drawer? Had I perhaps left the money in a pocket of my suit? I was convinced he didn't believe me. I told him I was wearing the same suit as I wore yesterday and that it was a habit of mine to empty my pockets when I got out of my suit. I was so cross with his apparent indifference that I pulled out the pockets of my suit to show him how I emptied my pockets each day. And then came my embarrassment. The five pound notes were in my trouser pocket!'

The following scene may appear in a dramatic script submitted to you by an author. Mechanize it for the studio, setting out any instructions required for the technical operator and the actors.

The scene is Yinka's office which is just off the general office of the Sapele Company. Yinka is on the telephone.
YINKA: This afternoon? Well, I'm not sure. Let me look at my diary. Yes, that'll be fine. What time? Two o'clock. Yes. See you then.
Tayo knocks on the door and enters.
YINKA: Come in!

TAYO: May I see you for a moment?

YINKA: I always have time to see you. Come in and sit down.

TAYO: I can't stay long, I'm expecting a phone call. I wanted to see you about the Budget File. Have you seen it recently?

YINKA: Not this week. I'll send for it.

Yinka rings a bell on his desk for the messenger.

TAYO: Macauley has it at present. Have you seen it since it was passed to him?

YINKA: No, I don't think so. No, I haven't seen it since last month now I come to think of it. Why?

TAYO: Well, there are a number of irregularities which I thought you ought to know about.

The messenger enters.

MESSENGER: You called, sir?

YINKA: Yes—go and ask Mr. Macauley for the Budget File.

The messenger turns to leave.

MESSENGER: Yes, sir.

YINKA: On second thoughts—ask Mr. Macauley to come and see me.

MESSENGER: Now, sir?

YINKA: Yes, now.

The messenger leaves.

TAYO: I'd better leave you alone with him.

Tayo rises to do so.

YINKA: Don't go far. I may need you.

TAYO: I'll be in my office. Just call.

Tayo leaves. Then the phone rings.

YINKA: Hello, yes.

The scene ends with music.

11   The talks programme

Talks were the earliest form of spoken word broadcasting. They are the simplest form and can still be the most effective. A good radio talk, well constructed and well delivered, can sparkle like a gem againstthe back ground of other programmes which make up the broadcast day. It can have all the authority of the printed word coupled with the warmth which comes from person to person contact.

In most broadcasting organizations the term 'talk' embraces the straightforward talk, the interview and the discussion. In some it also includes the documentary. In length a talk can range from a 1-minute contribution for a magazine programme to a 1-hour 'town meeting' with several featured speakers and audience participation. The trend these days is towards the shorter talk as research has shown the attention-span of the listener to be limited when one person alone is talking. The purpose of the talks programme may be to inform, to educate or simply to entertain.

As with all broadcasting, the intended audience must be clearly kept in mind. The programme intended for general listening has to be of popular appeal—the subject must be of wide general interest, the approach must be one which is commonly understood and the words must be the familiar words which everyone uses. The more specialist talk aimed at a particular audience need not be bound so tightly by these restrictions.

The personality of the speaker in a talks programme is of the greatest importance and far more so than in any other kind of programming. A dull personality seldom holds an audience even though his subject may be of great interest. It is sometimes unavoidable to use an otherwise unsuitable speaker but when this is so it is up to the producer to use his skill to the uttermost to make the speaker into an effective broadcaster. A wise talks producer builds up a panel of good personalities whom he can draw upon at any time.

The talk

The radio talk is neither a lecture nor a public address. The audience does not have to stay and listen nor can it see the speaker and be attracted by the way he uses his hands and his eyes. Everything in a radio talk has to be carried in the words: the familiar words we all use.

The best of radio talks is a friendly chat built around one subject. It is a spoken composition and like any composition it needs a unified structure: it has a clearly defined beginning, middle and an end. The words it uses are the action-words of everyday speech. It introduces the subject in an ear-catching way, explains it simply, develops its argument and then summarizes what it has said. Some talks producers reduce the structure of the talk to the following four phases: Begin to say it. Say it. Say it again. Say what you have said.

The writing of a radio talk should be lively, colourful and direct. It should not contain too many points. A well-prepared script is a 'slow' script in which the author has allowed himself sufficient time to make his points clearly and emphatically. The writing should be simple—too many unfamiliar or strange words may bolster a speaker's ego but they are likely to confuse and possibly irritate the listener. The speaker should not talk down to his listener nor should he assume him to be at his own level, and he should never try to demonstrate his own cleverness.

A radio talk should avoid statistics, using them sparingly if they must be used at all. Figures are best rounded out to easily understood whole numbers: 'a quarter of a million' is better than '238,784'.

Written shorthand has no place in a radio talk: 'and so on' is better than 'et cetera', 'namely' is better than 'viz', 'for example' is better than 'e.g.'. Some phrases should never be used. If a speaker says: 'I am going to prove to you . . .' he will appear arrogant and may antagonize his audience. Some words and phrases are distracting—'before I finish', 'in conclusion', 'if I had more time', 'a last word', 'finally' are all best avoided. We may be sorry that it is the end of an interesting talk or glad that it is the end of a dull one, but whether we are sorry or glad there is nothing to be gained by drawing attention to it. Fresh, vigorous writing is the making of a talk, not tired old clichés.

In the studio

Simple everyday psychology plays a part in the work of the talks producer in the studio. He has to learn to be a chameleon and change his colour to suit each speaker—flattering some, scolding others to get the performance he wants.

He should put his speaker at ease and encourage him to speak to the microphone as he would to a friend. Many talks producers find that it is a good idea to sit in the studio with a speaker, particularly if he is a newcomer to radio. He can then be encouraged to pitch his voice at the producer. His delivery will be more natural if he looks up from time to time at the producer, and by showing interest or otherwise the producer can encourage the speaker to work harder.

The production of a speaker who is over-selfconfident may be a problem for the producer for such people seldom like direction. To deal with the situation some producers record the talk without direction and then join the speaker in the studio for a play-back. By showing utter boredom and disinterest in the play-back the producer may then undermine the speaker's confidence; once this happens and the speaker asks, 'Could it have been better?' the producer has the opening he needs to offer direction and re-record the talk.

The interview

The radio interview is a lively variation of the talk. It considerably expands the potential pool of talks' contributors by bringing to the microphone people who have something to say but who cannot write talks or are too busy to do so. It is a popular form of talks broadcasting as most of us like to hear—or overhear—other people talking, and it is a very useful form particularly in countries where there are many languages and not all of them are understood by everyone.

Radio interviewing is not something any broadcaster can do. It requires a well-informed alert mind, a readiness with words and ideas, and an out-going gregarious personality. The shy broadcaster may be quite at home in the studio but he can never make a good interviewer.

There are several kinds of radio interview but essentially they can all be classified under two headings:
1. The personality interview which seeks to bring out the personality of the interviewee and tells us something about his life and ideas.
2. The information interview which seeks out facts.
The personality interview may be with or about a celebrity or someone whom we call a celebrity for the time being. It may show us how the interviewee thinks and feels, and how he reached his position in the public eye; it may bring out his views on questions of the day. This type of interview is generally slow moving and may be comparatively long. The technique of the personality interview is often used to present a character profile or portrait of a great man or woman. Sometimes it is used to bring a visiting celebrity before the public: a famous athlete or a popular entertainer.

The information interview is less interested in the personality of the interviewee than in what he has to tell us: about something that is in the news, some work he is engaged in or his views on an issue on which he is competent to talk. The interview usually moves along at a fair pace, with interviewer intruding little but simply holding up signposts, as it were, to keep the interviewee on the right track. The news interview, the magazine interview and the interview that is to form part of a documentary programme all belong in this category. This kind of interview is generally short—from 2 to 5 minutes—and it calls for particular skill on the part of the interviewer.

Preparing an interview

All interviews need careful preparation. They are not something which can be done quickly, off-the-cuff, except by experienced interviewers who work daily and consistently in this branch of broadcasting.

The preparation of an interview begins with research into the subject and the person to be interviewed. The more the interviewer knows about both, the better his interview will be. He need not be an authority on the subject but he must be well informed about it so as to devise pertinent questions and gain the respect of the interviewee—a matter of particular importance if the interviewee is an older man.

Suitable research material can be found in daily newspapers, magazines, encyclopaedias and pamphlets and papers published by government departments. Some interviewers like to know a good deal about the person they are interviewing and first approach his friends and associates for background material; this is particularly useful in the personality interview.

Once the research has been completed the interviewer can draw up a tentative list of questions—usually more than he intends to ask, their number of course depending upon the length of time allocated to the interview. Here again good talks practice should be followed—the interview should be about one subject only, and each question should uncover another facet of it. The best questions are those that an informed listener would ask, not irrelevant questions which simply waste time.

The devising of questions calls for skill. The right kind of question will start the interviewee talking whereas the wrong kind simply prompts a 'Yes' or 'No' answer. The interviewer should avoid putting all he knows about the subject into a question—his knowledge should only guide him to the right kind of question.

A bad question would be: 'I understand you've been working on this rural development programme in Ikete village for eight months and expect to be there for another six months before it is completed?' What can the interviewee say except 'Yes', or 'No, not another six months, we hope to finish it in four.'

A better question would be: 'How long have you been working on this rural development programme in Ikete village?' The interviewee now has something to bite into.

And better still: 'You've been working on the Ikete village rural development programme for six months—what has yet to be done before it's finished?' A question of this kind is likely to bring a very full answer, and the interviewer may need only to prompt the interviewee with one or two other questions to bring out the full story. The interviewer should avoid intruding if he can—the audience wants to hear the man or woman being interviewed not the interviewer himself. The interviewer is only a go-between, bringing the interviewee to the listener.

There is possibly one exception to this and that is where the interviewer is himself the programme. He may, for instance, be the regular compère of a weekly or daily interview programme, or an outstanding station personality whose opinions and views are valid and who is highly popular with the audience. The interviewer himself also makes the programme in field interviews where people may have little to say or lack the ability to say it. In such cases he may have interviewed the person in detail before beginning his broadcast and may then sum up what he has found out, turning to the interviewee only every now and again for 'Isn't that so?' or 'Am I right'. This technique can be useful also where the interviewee doesn't speak the language of the majority of the listeners.

The interviewer should refrain from making comments in the information interview, even unintentionally. 'I see . . .', 'Yes . . .', 'Would you believe it . . .' all imply a comment. The interview should progress from question to answer and from answer to a new question; there is seldom any need for linking phrases. Comments of any kind are particularly out of place in the news interview unless the purpose of the interview is to make news by pointing up shortcomings or inadequacies.

An interview should end with a good 'tag'—a strong point of argument or an amusing thought. The line of questioning should be prepared with this in view. A good tag makes an interview memorable and is likely to leave the listener thinking about what he has heard. If the tag is strong enough, and depending upon the culture of the country, there is little need for the otherwise weak 'thank you' at the end of an interview.

Field interviews

In conducting a field interview keep a sharp ear to the general acoustic background. Too much room echo or the low frequency rumble of traffic may distort the sound of the speaking voices and make it difficult for the listener to understand what is said. This is easily done by listening carefully to the over-all level of background and watching the deflections of the VU meter of the recorder before beginning the interview.

Where recording has to be done in an office, often the best position is to lean on a windowsill and speak out into the open air thus reducing the room resonance.

Sometimes background sound can be turned to good effect to make an interview sound more interesting and convey to the listener a picture of the scene.

A field interview at a dam site under construction may usefully begin with the sound of a near-by tractor at work. The interviewer could then begin: 'I'm standing right on the site of the new Volta dam just nearing completion. With me is the resident engineer, Mr. Xerly—Mr. Xerly what is that machine we can hear . . .?' And then progress to the intended questions.

Most microphones used for field recording have a wind shield to prevent puffs of wind moving the diaphragm and causing a disturbing rumble. Where a wind shield is not available one can often be improvised by draping several folds of a handkerchief or robe over the microphone. With the high quality equipment available nowadays there is no reason why the sound quality of a field recording should not equal that of a studio recording.

The discussion

The discussion programme provides a platform for the exchange of ideas. The ideas may be important ones which concern us as individuals, as members of a community or as nationals of a country; or they may be ideas intended simply to entertain us. The discussion may be serious or light-hearted, but its purpose is always to set us thinking.

The simplest discussion is an extension of the interview in which the interviewer plays a more positive or provocative role. He may present his own ideas so as to bring his guest out or perhaps to delve deeper into a subject. This kind of discussion is best handled by a station personality.

More conventional discussions are those presided over by a chairman and taking place between three or four participants; such panel discussions or forums are generally rather formal, with chairman acting as adjudicator or moderator and not participating in the discussion himself except to spark off a new line of inquiry. Usually one subject only is dealt with and it is examined in some depth, although in a variation of this type of programme several topics arising from listeners' letters may be discussed.

Still another type of discussion follows the lines of a debate and is usually held before an audience, either in the studio or in a public centre, perhaps as a town hall or a university auditorium. A chairman presides and two protagonists put forward opposing views on the question under debate, the audience being invited to join in their discussion. This type is popular in urban areas but it is also appropriate in rural districts.

The essential ingredient of any discussion is conflict. The members of the panel must have differing points of view. A discussion programme in which everyone agrees with everyone else makes very dull listening.

Discussion programmes are best organized in series—following the old radio axiom that the only way to build an audience is to put a programme on and keep it on.

Some discussion programmes with specific educational purposes invite listeners to form their own community discussion groups. These groups are sent circulars beforehand containing discussion group notes sketching the lines of the argument likely to be heard and suggesting questions for the groups to discuss. Results of these discussions are sometimes sent in to the radio station and points raised are then discussed from time to time in the programme series.

Preparing a discussion

The discussion programme needs the same careful preparation as a good interview.

The producer needs to research the subject and make very certain in his own mind that the subject is one that is capable of being discussed. Many discussion programmes fail because the subject is not one which will sustain discussion because it is of little concern to anyone or because there are not enough different points of view on the subject. In many broadcasting organizations the planning of discussion subjects is the work of a committee; committee discussion of programme subjects helps a producer to determine whether there are enough different points of view and often helps him to frame the question for a discussion.

The choice of subject has considerable bearing on the choice of participants, as does the way in which the question is put. For example: 'What kinds of people should our universities be producing?' A question of this kind is vague. Put in this way it is likely to interest only university staff. It may bring out many points of view without any hope of general agreement.

'Do we need more lawyers or more practical engineers?' This is a better approach to what may be the same question but again would limit the discussion and the choice of speakers. It is a question for lawyers, economists and engineers.

'Would you advise your son to be a lawyer or an engineer?' This is a far broader question and one that is likely to stimulate immediate listener interest. It offers scope for discussion of national objectives, views on the present situation and discussion of employment opportunities. It immediately suggests possible participants—an engineer, a lawyer, a prominent women's leader, a graduate who feels that he has entered the wrong calling.

All discussions need careful planning. The subject of the discussion must be of interest to the audience for whom it is intended. The subject must be thoughtfully chosen, and the microphone personalities of the participants should be carefully considered.

Producing the discussion

The producer should talk with all the participants to learn about their points of view before arranging his rehearsal. A brief typed summary of these should be given to the chairman who should also have an opportunity to talk with the participants himself before the recording is made.

During the rehearsal the chairman and the producer should find out which of the participants is likely to have the most to say on any particular aspect of the subject. The producer should then note the amount of time which each stage of the discussion is likely to require, and prepare a running-sheet indicating time from a 00.00 minutes start. During the recording he can then signal these 'time gates' to the chairman as each one is reached.

He should brief the speakers carefully, showing them how to face up to the microphone and he should point out the difficulties which arise from 'over-talking'—that is breaking in on a speaker and talking at the same time as he is talking. The best way is for a participant to raise a hand or an eyebrow to the chairman when he wants to cut in. The chairman can then let one participant complete his idea before calling in another. In this way a good chairman can control a discussion without taking any of the life out of it. In the early part of a programme the chairman should name the speakers frequently until the listener is able to identify them by voice.

It is well to pay special attention to the placing of participants, particularly if the studio lacks a round table. If the only table available is a long one it is better to put the more effusive speakers at the ends. When shy speakers are seated at the extremes of a table they tend to take comfort in their isolation and fail to contribute freely to the discussion.

Note pads, pencils and glasses of water should be provided for each participant.

Most discussions end with a summary from the chairman. It is important that this be purely a summary and not a speech in which the chairman airs his own views or raises new questions which have not been touched upon in the general discussion.

General

From the talks programme have been derived nearly all the other forms of spoken word broadcasting—the educational programme for schools, the documentary, the magazine, special programmes for particular audiences— children, farmers, women. It is a very basic form of broadcasting and one which, in a sense, existed long before radio began. The talk, the interview and the discussion are all part of our daily lives.

We all talk to someone giving our views on topics of the day and about things we see. We all ask and are asked questions—about ourselves, about the things we do, about the things we want to do, about what we know and about what we want to know. We discuss our ideas and our plans with other people —members of our families, our friends and our associates. We join together in groups at village and town meetings, in councils and in parliaments to discuss our ideas and to prepare plans for action.

The best of radio talks programming is simply an extension of the talking we do in our everyday lives. The talks producer should, therefore, be guided by the talks activity of his own people. If in his own society there are meetings of elders and tribal meetings he should try to find ways of adapting these to radio, particularly in provincial vernacular broadcasting. It is only by working through the existing framework of society that radio can help to broaden our ideas and put distant peoples in touch with one another.

The kinds of talks programming sketched in this chapter are the conventional ones which have been tried and proved elsewhere, but they are not the only ones. In the English-speaking radio world the formal talk began in Britain, the interview in the United States of America, the town meeting and rural forum in Canada. They have changed over the years and been adopted in various forms by broadcasters in other parts of the world. In each case they entered into radio because they were means of communication which were already known outside of radio; the radio listener was familiar with the technique. As radio reaches out to other lands it must adapt itself to other people and take its programme inspiration from the way other people think and live. To do its job radio must be vitally and closely related to the lives of its listeners and not to the lives of listeners in some distant country.

Action projects

The short talk and the short interview are always more difficult than the long talk and the long interview. Train yourself in both by doing the following:

1. Prepare a talk of 2½ minutes duration on a subject with which you are familiar—perhaps about your job or how and why you began a career in broadcasting.
2. Prepare a talk of up to 10 minutes on a subject requiring research—something in history, something about your customs, or about a new civic proposal or development.
3. Prepare and record a short interview of 3-minute duration with one of your classmates or one of your station's personalities.
4. Visit your city or town market and prepare a 6-minute descriptive item which includes an interview with a market vendor or the market inspector.

Play back and evaluate these projects with other members of your class. Was the material well organized, was the message clear? How could they have been improved?

Class discussion projects

1. Examine the ways in which your station uses talks programming. Are they the best ways for your listeners? Do they relate to the audience?
2. Where and for what reasons in your community do people come together and talk? How are the meetings organized? Who sits in the chair? What is discussed? Are there established precedents for speaking? Can these meetings be adapted to broadcasting and used as the idea for a series of radio programmes?

12 The news programme

Radio offers the fastest means of disseminating news. The radio news bulletin reaches people in remote country areas hours and sometimes days before the arrival of a city newspaper. For many people radio is their only source of news.

News is important to all of us because it keeps us informed as to what is happening in our own community and what is happening in other communities which impinge upon our own. It satisfies our curiosity and concern and it provides us with basic facts which enable us to make up our minds and so join in the general discussion which leads to community action.

Man has always had a need for news. In past times and in isolated remote communities the gathering and transmission of news was haphazard. The reconnoitring hunter saw a herd of game and reported it to his fellow hunters. The emissary in a foreign territory heard of the warlike intentions of a neighbouring clan and reported the fact to his elders at home. The women of a village found a new edible plant and told their families and friends about it. Armed with such information, the hunters, the elders, the women could develop plans of action. The information they gathered and news of the action they were likely to take were passed on farther afield through talking drums and in the songs of the town-crier. And so the news was spread.

Our news needs have grown with our societies. Today we need to know not only what is happening in and about our own village—although this is still very important—but we also need to know what is happening in our own capital city, what is happening in neighbouring countries and what is happening in far distant countries.

We may live in a village by a river. We may hear in the news that the government of our country in the capital city has agreed with a neighbouring country to build a large dam on the river which serves us. We may have fears that damming of the river will reduce the amount of water available and endanger our flood-land crops or destroy the fish of the river. Because we have heard the news we are able to discuss it with our village elders and urge them to take the matter up with the government in the city. The government may not listen to what we have to say, but we have heard also that the pro-

96

, posed dam is to be financed by a foreign government. We may write to that government and put our case. Finally our views may be heard—and all because of the news.

What is news?

In a word—everything. Everything that has happened recently which we have not yet heard about and everything which is about to happen.

A famous publisher once said: 'When a dog bites a man that isn't news, but when a man bites a dog that is news.' He was referring to sensational news but an event does not have to be sensational to be news. It just has to happen and to be of sufficient concern to people. If the publisher's dog had rabies it would be important to the man, his family and neighbours. If there were no medical services available it would be all the more important.

All news is important but there are orders of importance in news. The news which generally interests us most is local news—news about people we know and news about happenings and proposals which are likely to have an immediate and direct effect on our own lives.

The news which a radio station broadcasts or a newspaper publishes is not all the news of the hour or of the day. It is selected news—news which in the news editor's experience has some importance to listeners and readers.

Gathering news

News is collected by reporters—men and women trained in the collection and interpretation of facts. They are people who know their own communities very well. Many of them have specialist spheres of interest in community affairs: politics, the work of government departments, law, transport, communications. The modern journalist is highly informed about many matters and is exceptionally well read. He has an intuitive flair for picking up half-formulated ideas and giving them definition.

Radio gets its news from several sources. Some large stations employ a number of journalists—sometimes called 'leg men' because they have much walking to do to collect their stories. Others cull their news from newspapers and often by arrangement with the newspapers. Nearly all radio stations subscribe to one or more of the many international news agencies, sometimes called wire services, which have reporters around the world and who sell their news to interested buyers.

The basis of a news story is often said to be found in the following words: What? Where? Who? When? Why? How?

What happened, where did it happen, who did it happen to, when did it happen, why did it happen and how did it happen?

It is a good formula for working out any news story as it puts the questions uppermost in our minds into a logical order.

The production broadcaster is not ordinarily concerned in news and news gathering although news touches on many phases of his work. But he should know that his newsroom or news editor is likely to be interested in any worthwhile story he comes across.

Two kinds of news

Journalists sometimes speak of two kinds of news:

Hard news, which is the reporting of important events which have taken place. A speech by a leading political figure, an important government announcement, a crime, a disaster, a significant court verdict—these all come under the heading of hard news and will surely find their way into the news bulletin.

Soft news, which is news of a more informational nature and not as immediate or, in the opinion of a news editor, as important as hard news. Much of the material used in a magazine programme and in some talks can be put in the category of soft news. The programme broadcaster is, therefore, much concerned with soft news.

The news bulletin

News bulletins have assumed increasing importance in radio broadcasting in recent years. In the early days of radio there was seldom more than one bulletin a day and it was broadcast after the evening newspapers reached the streets and had been sold. As radio stations built up their own news staffs the number of bulletins increased. Many stations today have several long bulletins interspersed with hourly or even half-hourly news summaries.

Where there are several bulletins in a day it is important that the bulletins change or appear to change. The same bulletin heard several times with the stories assembled in the same way and in exactly the same words is likely to rob radio of its news importance.

The stories in a news bulletin are usually assembled in order of importance. Sometimes prominence is given to local or national stories, with sports news and some human interest story to round the bulletin off.

Reading the news bulletin

News reading is generally the preserve of a station's leading and clearest announcers. The news reader should be well informed and familiar with the background to every story that he reads. If a story fails to make sense to him it will certainly not make sense to his listeners. He should know accurately the pronunciation of all words which appear in the bulletin—words in everyday speech and the names of places and people appearing in the news.

Some radio stations use two news readers alternating with each other. In this way the stories are separated from each other so that there is little likelihood of confusion in the listener's mind. Other stations use a gong stroke or an electronic 'pip' to separate stories. A drum beat could be similarly used.

If you are concerned with news reading, you should refer again to the chapter on microphone talent.

Does the message get across?

Because news bulletins are presented in the way they are it does not follow that the accepted method is the best or only method. It is simply one that has grown up with the years and in societies where there are many outlets for news information.

Does the formal presentation of a news bulletin really get the message across to listeners—particularly listeners in the less sophisticated villages?

At least one African broadcaster doubts the value of presenting news without at the same time overtly drawing attention to its significance. In traditional African society news information and education are interrelated. The village-crier not only says what has happened and why but he also points to the significance of what he has to say and draws a moral from it: 'A woman has died of fever because she refused to go to the hospital. Now let everyone hear this—if you have a fever, brother, please don't hesitate to go to the hospital or the same thing may happen to you.' The village-crier is not only giving the news he is also giving a useful and pertinent comment on it.

Can this traditional style be adapted to broadcasting? The news broadcaster is only a village-crier with a larger voice.

There are precedents in radio of this kind. In the United States several famous newscasters won their reputations because they not only read the news but commented on it at the same time so that listeners could better understand and appreciate the significance of the news.

The question, 'Does the message get across?', is one that a broadcaster should always ask himself. We apply it to other forms of broadcasting: why not ask it of the news?

The newsreel

It is more usual to separate comment from the news by including it in news talks and newsreels. The daily newsreel of fifteen or more minutes duration is a popular form of news broadcasting. It contains eye-witness accounts, extracts of speeches and reports of other events, commentaries, short talks and interviews in much the same way as a newspaper includes pictures and feature articles.

The newsreel is expensive to produce as it requires a large staff, good communication and other technical facilities if it is to be professionally made. It is beyond the capacity of a small station with insufficient finance and staff. The editor must be able to select what he wishes to use from a large number of items and a good newsreel calls also for skilled tape editing and well-written link narrations. Some points about these are made in the next chapter.

As alternative to the full newsreel occasional sound excerpts may be included in a normal news bulletin. A speech by a leading dignitary reported in the news can be highlighted by the inclusion of a 20- or 30-second extract which illustrates the manner and personality of the speaker. A news report of a sporting event, say a football game, may end with live sound of the last few seconds of play, the commentator's cry of 'Goal!' and the roar of the crowd.

The integrated news broadcast

Another technique in news presentation is the half-hour news broadcast once a day. This 30-minute period includes a formal bulletin, several newsreel items and one or two commentaries. The time given to each element varies according to the importance and news value of available items.

In theory the half-hour is divided into equal thirds: bulletin, magazine material and commentary. In practice, however, the time may be divided into 4 minutes of hard news bulletin, 16 minutes of magazine interviews and reports, and approximately 10 minutes commentary—the commentary period may cover both local events and world affairs. Another day the time may be allotted differently with more hard news, a single magazine item and longer commentaries.

Such lengthy news presentation assumes considerable interest in news on the part of listeners and willingness to sit and listen for a long period of time.

The general trend, however, is towards shorter and more frequent news broadcasts with the emphasis in each short bulletin concentrated on items likely to be of interest to an audience tuned in at that specific time. Early morning news is designed for a general audience, mid-morning for a predominantly women's audience, mid-day for farmers, late afternoon for young mothers and children, returning to a general audience at night and a more sophisticated audience at late night.

The only sure formula is the one which works for your listeners.

Action projects

1. Survey the news outlets available to listeners in your area. How many daily newspapers are published? What are their circulation figures (number of copies printed and sold each day)? How does the total circulation of the available newspapers compare with the estimated audience for your station's news bulletins?
2. What do you know about your station's news organization—what are the sources of its news? Do the bulletins change frequently—are new stories added, is the wording of old stories up-dated?
3. Compare on a percentage basis the amount of space in your local newspapers and the amount of time on your station given to hard and soft news.

Class discussion

Does your station give sufficient time to news? Is it effectively presented—does it get the message across? What is the class's reaction to a pattern of news presentation based on the technique of the village-crier? To what extent in your home community are news information and education tradition-ally interrelated?

13   Documentary and magazine programmes

There is a large field of spoken word programming which cannot readily be categorized as news, talks or drama but which has the truth and urgency of news and uses the techniques of talks and drama. It is factual broadcasting, specifically informational in character and often directly educational in intent. The word 'documentary' is frequently used to describe it.

The word documentary is derived from the French *documentaire* and was first coined by early film-makers to describe a school of film-making which was neither wholly fictional nor wholly factual. The documentaries which these film-makers produced probed pertinently into the nature of human society and frequently made acid comments on human behaviour and government.

The style of the documentary film attracted broadcasters who saw in it an exciting way to make radio more alive and interesting. It appealed to talks producers who were tired of the limitations of the studio talk, it appealed to outside broadcasters who believed that radio could do more than report sports events, and it appealed to drama producers who believed ahead of their time that drama could be more realistic. The early radio documentaries strongly reflected the techniques of the talk, the outside broadcast and the drama. They were usually made in the studio for lack of suitable compact field recording equipment—the tape recorder had not been developed at the time—and they relied upon actors to play all the speaking roles. It was not long after its development that the documentary—complete with scripts, actors, mood music and sound effects—ventured beyond the studio. Producers began to stage documentaries as live outside broadcasts from museums, factories and national monuments; they added live short talks and interviews to help get the story across. It was then that the use of the documentary was seen as a teaching medium and many documentary producers embarked on series of adult educational broadcasts as the forerunners of schools broadcasting.

With the arrival of the portable recorder (it was at first a disc recorder) the newsreel programme emerged. It found ready imitators in other kinds of magazine programmes for sectional audiences. Documentary producers adopted some newsreel and magazine techniques—they began to use more 'real people' and fewer actors—and since then the magazine and the documentary have become very much alike—so much so, in some instances, that it is difficult to tell the two apart.

This brief account of the evolution of the documentary and the magazine may be helpful to producers who sometimes find the differences confusing. The two types of programmes can be differentiated if we remember that the purpose of the documentary is to educate in a vigorous and stimulating way while that of the magazine is to inform.

The production techniques of both the documentary and the magazine are used in many schools broadcasts and other directly instructional and teaching programmes.

The documentary producer

Documentary is a field for the very experienced producer who, preferably, has a journalistic flair. This does not mean to say that he has to be a journalist but he needs a journalist's ability to collect and evaluate facts. He also needs the dramatist's bent for displaying facts dramatically and building excitement and suspense into his programme. It is for lack of this latter quality that journalists sometimes fail in the field of documentary.

A good capacity for research, a thorough knowledge of the technical facilities of radio, skill in tape editing and writing talent are essential attributes of the documentary producer.

The documentary programme

The documentary programme is a story of something. It is generally between 15 and 60 minutes in length—the actual length is usually related to the size of the subject and the way in which it is treated. An industrial or agricultural development may warrant up to 30 minutes, while a historical re-enactment or archive programme (that is one using previously recorded historical material) may require 45 or 60 minutes.

The critical questions for the producer to ask himself when embarking on a documentary programme are:
1. What length will the subject interestingly sustain?
2. What techniques can I use to hold listener interest over a long period?
There are many types of documentary programmes. Most are factual—that is they are concerned with real things. But some are abstract—they are extensions of reality or they probe into hidden regions beyond reality. What I do is real, what I think is abstract.

The documentary can tell the story of something that is happening or that has happened. It may tell of an important national event about to take place, or one that did take place in the past. It can tell us about the life of a person, what he did and what he thought. It can interpret the world about us and teach us something about it. It may tell us about the way other peoples live. It may show us how things happen—how a farmer works, how a shoe is made, what a bank does. It may inquire into a social problem and point towards solutions.

But whatever the subject or the type of documentary it must be entertaining as well as educational. If it is not entertaining people will just not listen.

The documentary technique

The documentary uses sound to tell its story—the sound of the human voice, the sound of human activity and the sound of music.

The main character in most documentaries is the narrator. Some very successful documentaries use only a narrator and rely upon the imagery of his speech to tell the story. This technique is used mainly in the shorter documentaries which, if the narration is imaginatively written and dramatically told, can be highly effective, particularly with children and less-sophisticated audiences. The choice of the narrator, the warmth and personality of his voice are very important. Narration in the documentary is not news-reading or link-announcing: it is story-telling.

The narration-only documentary is not limited to speech. It can use lyric verse, backed by music, to get its story across. The songman and the troubadour were the narrators of old, long before radio was invented, and they are still important in many societies today. The tradition of the songman can be adapted to radio and it is well suited to vernacular documentary programming.

In addition to the narrator the documentary also uses actors and the voices of real people. It may combine all three in one programme.

Actors may play the parts of people who are no longer alive or are living too far away to be recorded; or they can act for people who cannot speak at the microphone because of impediments or because their languages are not understood. They can also re–enact dialogue—dialogue which actually took place or which has been invented by the producer to explain a situation or portray an event. They may also be used to express the views of people who do not really exist—the man in the street, the 'typical' house-wife, the 'typical' farmer and so on. They can even speak for animals and objects—birds, walls, trees, mountains.

The voices of real people are generally heard in short extracts culled from talks and interviews, carefully edited and interspersed in the narration.

The documentary uses all these devices together with mood music and sound effects to tell its story. The flow between narration, sound and other voices needs careful plotting.

Making the documentary

The first stage in making a documentary is research. The writer-producer needs to know the subject thoroughly. This work may be done in the library, by reading through newspaper files and by talking to people concerned in the subject of the programme. In the course of his research the writer forms some ideas as to how different parts of the programme are to be treated—in narration, interview, or acted out in dialogue.

Many documentary writers write the story of their programme in two or three thousand words after they have completed their research and then put it aside for several weeks. When they return to it and read their material again a whole new approach may become apparent.

Once the research is completed—whether it has been written out as a story or not—the next step is to express the object and substance of the programme in a short sentence.

Take this sentence as an example: 'A change in the social framework of our villages is the first step to improved agriculture.'

This précis may stimulate some ideas for a title to the programme: 'New Ideas, Better Crops', 'Change for the Future', 'The Old Village Must Go!', 'Not as in Grandad's Day', 'Think and Grow Yams'.

The sequences of the programme can then be planned as an expansion of the simple short statement.

1. How the present social framework hampers the introduction of new ideas. Some examples.
2. An example of a village which increased its productivity and income by introducing new methods.
3. What needs to be done to change the social framework—the importance of the school, the support of the agricultural extension officer.
4. The first steps to bring about change.
5. Re-statement of the benefits of change.
6. Who opposes change. Is it possible to change the views of the opponents. How?
7. Can this be done in your village?

When the sequence plan has been developed and tested against the research it is then possible to examine and decide upon the techniques to be used in each sequence:

1. Narration, with additional voice to give the examples (2 minutes).
2. Actuality recordings from village 'A' (4 minutes).
3. Narration and short talks by three specialists (6–7 minutes).
4. Narration (2 minutes).
5. Cuts from actuality recordings made in village 'A' (3 minutes).
6. Interviews in village 'B' (3 minutes).
7. Narration and interviews from village 'B' or narration leading to short discussion between officers appearing in sequence 3 (5–6 minutes).

By breaking down the subject into a series of sequences and plotting the style of treatment and approximate time of each sequence it is possible for the producer to 'see' the likely final shape of his programme. While doing this some ideas for the words and phrases to be used in the narration are likely to occur. They should be noted on the sequence plan.

The planning of the documentary, along the lines indicated above, is best done on a large sheet of double-fold ledger paper. Working from left to right across the page it is then possible to plan out the programme. The first entry on the left-hand side of the page is the short précis of the programme; then column by column the enlargement of the idea with the final column containing notes for narration lines, summaries of recorded inserts and the running time of the inserts. It is from this final column that the actual script is written.

Some documentary producers have found from experience that at certain times in a half-hour programme audience interest is likely to wane unless something new or exciting happens in the programme to sustain the interest. They plan to use music breaks or new voices or exciting ideas or sounds at these 'danger points'. Timing from a oo.oo minutes start of programme the danger points are: 3, 5, 8, 16, 21 and 27 minutes.

Good planning is never more necessary than in the documentary programme. The plan will show clearly whether the idea will sustain a programme, and it will also indicate how to go about making the programme.

The documentary series

The radio documentary is generally best programmed as a series. Several series may be run at the same time. Each series should be under the control of a senior producer who may have several writers and researchers working for him. With this method of programme organization the best use can be made of the teaching potential of the documentary.

Each series should have a featured narrator who preferably is heard only in that series. The personality of the narrator will then help to build up a loyal following.

The different series can be devoted to national development in education, industry and agriculture; to the history and culture of the nation; to government and current affairs.

The magazine programme

The regular radio magazine programme, derived from the newsreel, is a useful outlet for a great deal of informational and soft news material which cannot be programmed elsewhere.

Magazine programmes vary in length; usually either 15 or 30 minutes. They consist of short talks, interviews, on-the-spot reports and eye-witness accounts of events, commentaries, music and sometimes poetry and short stories.

The longer magazines are generally aimed at a wide audience while the shorter magazines are usually intended for special audiences—women, school-teachers, farmers, businessmen, students and listeners having a special interest in science, art or hobbies.

The items in the short magazine programme seldom are longer than two-and-a-half minutes. Thus a 15 ½ minute magazine may have four or five separate items. The length of item in the longer magazine is usually between 3 and 4 ½ minutes. The shorter the items the quicker the pace of the programme. A fast moving programme appeals to urban listeners whereas rural listeners generally expect a more leisurely pace but there are no fixed rules. The producer must understand his audience and pace the programme accordingly.

Assembling the magazine programme

Careful consideration needs to be given to the placing of items in the magazine programme—and in this regard it is useful to remember the 'danger points' referred to in the section on documentary.

The better magazines generally open with a short and topical item to catch the listener's interest. Weightier material is best held in reserve for use about two-thirds of the way through the programme. Lighter—often story or humorous material—is customarily used at the end of a magazine programme.

Some of the longer magazine programmes make use of music either as a comment on material or a bridge between items. Music can also make a complete item in a programme—the 'top of the week' or a regular song-spot. But it is not good practice to use music simply because there is no other apparent way to separate or link two items.

The same narrator should be used for each edition of a magazine programme. He gives it a stamp and identity of its own much in the same way as the 'flag' or title of a printed magazine identifies it amongst many magazines on a news-stand.

Transitions or link-continuity

The narrator's lines in a magazine are called link-continuity or transitions.

Link writing should be interesting and natural. It should tell us what we need to know about what is to follow and it should appear to make the magazine 'hold together'. Where the link-continuity is good there is little need for music bridges between items.

Let us say we have two items in a science magazine. One has been a talk about a new insecticide and it is to be followed by another talk about heart surgery. A very bald and poor link would be: 'That was Doctor X talking about a newly developed insecticide. Now here is a talk about new developments in heart surgery by Doctor Y.'

Such a link can be made much more interesting; for example: 'A new insecticide may be bad news for beetles but it's good news for us. And more good news in science is the rapid progress in heart surgery at the ABC hospital. Here's Doctor Y to bring us up to date with the latest developments.'

In a general magazine with two on-the-spot reports following one another we may write the link this way: 'While reporter Chwukuma Okeke was out at the sports stadium this afternoon, Saula Fadike went to look at the work being done on the new shipping terminal. This million-pound development should be completed by the end of the year. As Fadike says, it's an impressive step forward which will profit each one of us. . . .'

Sometimes in link-continuity it is a good idea to give listeners a 'picture' of the person who is about to speak: 'Mrs. Mary Omolu is a tireless worker in the cause of women's rights. A tall, very dignified woman, she was dressed in a fine blue cotton wrap-around and brilliant yellow head-tie when we called on her this afternoon to talk about her new campaign.'

Good link writing and good transitions make a programme lively.

A magazine script should include all that is necessary for the technical operator and the narrator to know. The in and out cues of tape inserts and the duration of the inserts should be clearly marked on the script:

(TAPE *Fadike*):
BEGINS 'The port officer told me that the estimated increase . . .'
ENDS '. . . in the record time of one year and two months' (*Time:* 2'07")

Where the same cue appears twice, the script should carry a warning note to this effect to avoid the danger of an operator accidentally cutting the insert ahead of time.

Where pronunciations are likely to be difficult or unfamiliar the script should include guides for the narrator: '. . . Mr. Farlaytoi (rhymes with CHARLEY-BOY)' ; '. . . the Finnish capital of Helsinki (HEL•sinki).'

Action projects

1. Study the documentary film and compare it with the documentary radio programme. If the government of your country supports a documentary film unit, arrange to see a number of its productions: do the objectives of these films parallel in any way the objectives of your station's radio documentaries? What are the differences and the similarities in technique?

2. Plan a radio documentary which has a relevant social purpose. The subject may have to do with community welfare or a current national project. Put the plan into action and make the programme. Audition the programme to your class and evaluate its effectiveness.

3. Analyse a popular printed magazine. What kind of reading public is it intended for? What kinds of stories does it publish? What is the relative prominence given to the different stories? Compare the stories and the space given to them with the stories and time given to topics in a radio magazine broadcast by your station.

4. Summarize the stories printed in the magazine chosen for project 3. If these stories were to be used in a radio magazine, in what order would you use them? Write suitable link-continuity for the stories chosen.

Class discussions

1. Do you agree that the purpose of the documentary is primarily to educate while that of the magazine programme is to inform?
2. Do you think that the quick appearance of many stories in a magazine programme on radio can sometimes confuse the audience? How can you avoid this confusion?

Most radio programming is intended for a general audience, but increasing use is being made of the medium to offer special groups of listeners specifically educational programmes.

This use of radio is particularly well suited to developing countries where means of communication and transport are often poor and there are seldom enough teachers, public health and welfare officers, adult education and agricultural extension workers. Radio provides an exceptionally inexpensive means of conveying knowledge and information and, in the view of some authorities, this use of broadcasting is radio's most significant contribution towards the achievement of national developmental objectives.

Programmes for sectional audiences

The general audience for radio can be subdivided into many groups of people having certain common needs and interests. Once identified, these groups can become target audiences for special programmes designed for organized group or community listening.

The three most readily identified of these groups are: children at school, adults in search of further education, men and women in rural communities.

Children at school

Most educationists and broadcasters are agreed that educational radio is no substitute for the class-room teacher, but that it can assist the teacher in the class-room in many ways. It can appeal to a child's imagination and extend the horizons of his mind. It is particularly helpful in providing support for the teacher in social-science subjects, and in language teaching it can provide models which the teacher may not be able to provide himself.

Schools broadcasts are generally planned in association with the State Ministry of Education, and they are scheduled to parallel the teaching curriculum throughout each term and the school year. Sometimes ministries of education engage special radio officers either to advise the broadcasters or to produce the programmes for the broadcasters to use. For successful schools broadcasting, close collaboration between educational authorities and broad-casters is essential from the planning stage to the point of reception of the broadcasts. Meetings between programme producers and the educational authorities at every level from the ministry to the teacher in his class-room should be held frequently. The teacher can also be of special help to the pro-gramme producer by reporting back on the success or failure of the broad-cast programme.

The more the teacher knows about a coming schools broadcast the more likely is he to use the broadcast, therefore very full notes for teachers concern-ing every schools broadcast are sent out to schools well in advance of the term and before the start of the series of broadcasts. The notes may draw attention to the specific teaching points to be made in each broadcast or they can provide teachers with references to additional background material and possi-bly some diagrams where illustration is likely to make the radio lesson more effective.

As a follow-up to the schools broadcast, many broadcasting organi-zations employ special liaison officers who visit schools to observe how teachers use the broadcast in the class-room. Regular visits by liasion officers help to keep producers informed about reception conditions, the effectiveness of the programmes and the manner in which teachers use the programmes.

Techniques in schools broadcasting

The techniques of the talks programme with discussions and interviews, and those of the documentary and the magazine, are all used in the production of educational broadcasts.

The tempo of a direct teaching programme is, however, generally slower than that of a comparable general broadcast. More time is given to recapitula-tion. The slower pacing of narration takes stock of the fact that acoustics are often poor in the class-room. It is usual to seek out particularly clear voices to play the speaking parts, and greater consideration is given to the distinctions between one voice and another.

It must be remembered however that a schools broadcast is still a broadcast and if it is to hold its audience it must be vital and interesting. The child in the class-room may not be able to switch off the radio set but he can quickly lose interest and 'switch off his ears'.

Adults in search of further education

We all seek to enlarge our education and much of the daily programme mat-erial of any radio station helps us to do this. There are, however, special groups of people who have particular needs which radio can serve parti-cularly well.

A few moments thought about your own community will prompt you to make a sizeable list of such groups: young mothers, market vendors, students of shorthand, youngsters leaving school, small-businessmen, motorists and truck drivers, farmers and public officials of many kinds. All these groups, and many others, constitute potential audiences for special educational and informative programmes. This is particularly true in developing countries where other mass media are less well developed than radio and where newspapers and films fail to reach the nationwide audiences reached by radio.

Many kinds of teaching programmes can be developed for these sectional groups. Often such programmes may parallel schools broadcasts—where for instance government literacy programmes are operating, or where there are special public health and similar campaigns.

Many of these groups can be reached by special magazine programmes directed to a particular audience. An example of such a special programme allied to schools broadcasting is the radio magazine for teachers, a weekly programme designed to overcome the sense of isolation often experienced by teachers in remote areas. A programme of this kind can keep teachers in touch with one another; it can provide a forum for the discussion of problems facing teachers, and it can help teachers to broaden their understanding of their own profession.

Where a radio station serves a large city it can give group identity and provide special services for men and women at work in particular callings. For example, many young men and women are today studying shorthand in an attempt to get ahead in the clerical professions. Two 10-minute programmes a week of local news read at dictation speed can be of great use to such people. Where there are good relations between broadcaster and newspaper editors the texts of the broadcasts can later be printed in the newspapers so that listeners may correct their own dictation.

Programmes of this kind put radio to use to serve the community.

Programmes for rural communities

A notable achievement in community broadcasting is the rural radio forum, a special kind of programme for farmers and villagers. It is a type of magazine programme but which allows for two-way traffic between the broadcaster and the listener.

The rural radio forum which began in Canada and has subsequently spread to many countries has shown that radio can make a significant contribution to the communities it serves.

The rural radio forum is a style of programming which provides for organized village listening by groups of fifteen to twenty villagers who assemble weekly around a community receiver and under the direction of a chairman. The station broadcasts a regular series of 30- to 45-minute programmes specially for these groups. A programme may deal with a number of subjects or it may be devoted to a single subject. The subjects are always those of particular interest to rural communities: agriculture, health, nutrition, village government and social questions. Various techniques are used: the talk, discussion, drama. At the end of each broadcast the chairman leads discussion concerned with the principal subject of the broadcast. The chairman or a group secretary reports back to the station by letter on the conclusions reached by the group; he asks questions which the group would like to hear answered in subsequent broadcasts and suggests topics for future broadcasts.

Experiments in rural radio forums in India and Ghana were organized in association with government agencies concerned with social education, village welfare and agriculture. Officers of the various agencies assisted in the organization of the groups at the village level and frequently acted as secretaries for the listening groups. The broadcasters planned the topics in discussion with various ministries of government, and together with the ministries evaluated the results. The results have been impressive.[1]

The producer and the special programme

The educational and informative programmes discussed in this chapter involve the producer much more closely with specialists than does general broadcasting. In planning, preparation and production he must consult with, and seek the co-operation of, public officials in several categories.

There is considerable debate in many broadcasting organizations as to whether or not the producers of these kinds of special programmes should be specialists themselves. Should a producer of schools broadcasts have at some time in his career been a teacher himself? Or should he first be a broadcaster who has later studied the problems peculiar to schools broadcasting? The question has not yet been completely resolved.

But no matter what the producer's background it is essential that he have a special interest in the area in which he is working and a particular sympathy for the subject. He should regard contributors to his programmes very much as co-workers and should spend more than the normal amount of time explaining to them the difficulties and techniques of broadcasting. By co-operating with his contributors he can learn a great deal about his audience, its needs and its reactions to the programmes.

Action projects

1. If your station carries schools broadcasts make a study of a particular series. Listen to the broadcasts and assess their worth. Attend a school which is using these programmes and study the way in which the teacher uses them. Try to discover whether children in the class-room have profited from the teaching points and the extent to which they have done so.
2. List the special audiences which your station could serve in its own community. Does the station carry programmes of special value to these

1. *Radio Broadcasting Serves Rural Development* and *An African Experiment in Radio Forums for Rural Development*, Paris, Unesco, 1965, 1968 (Reports and Papers on Mass Communication, 48 and 51).

audiences? Can you suggest other types of special programmes for sectional audiences?

3. Arrange to discuss the work and objectives of some public officials who spend their lives in the field with officers of their departments. Discover what they think about radio and the extent to which it can serve them.

15   Light entertainment programmes

Not all radio programming is serious or of vital social concern. A great number of hours are set aside simply for entertainment and these are the hours which build the popularity of radio and win and hold audiences.

Light entertainment is a rather loose term used by many stations to cover a wide field of programming: book and short story readings; serialized drama, particularly light and humorous drama; variety programmes featuring light musical entertainment, comics, community singing; some types of listeners' letter programmes; quizzes and panel games.

The more common types of light entertainment are variety programmes, quizzes and panel games. They are usually staged before live audiences in cinemas and public halls, and sometimes in studios where the station has a suitably large studio. The presence of an audience does much to add to the spirit of a variety programme.

Variety programmes

The success of a variety entertainment is largely dependent upon the amount of talent available. And although some countries are better off than others in this respect, almost everywhere there is some talent available for the light entertainment producer to bring into broadcasting.

In many African communities established country theatre and singing parties already enjoy wide popularity in rural areas. These groups attract natural entertainers and comics who express some aspects of traditional culture and they deserve the larger audience which radio can give them.

The amateur talent quest is one type of programme which uncovers new talent and helps raise the entertainment standard. Selected amateurs —vocalists, musicians, bands, choirs, story-tellers—are invited to take part in series of competitions and their performances are judged by the studio audience. The programme series may be staged in many towns and district centres until finally national winners are selected.

Quiz and panel games

The quiz programme and the panel game are both good audience builders. They have been very successful in many countries although their audiences have declined with the introduction of television. Some African light entertainment producers have introduced them with success to African audiences.

There are many kinds of quiz programmes ranging from the more serious general knowledge quiz to the lighter programme played mainly for laughs. The idea on which a quiz or panel game is based is called the format.

The more serious type of quiz takes the form of a competition either between individual contestants or groups of contestants representing schools, employees of large institutions (banks, government departments, railways, ports authorities), towns and districts. The 'spelling bee' is an early and still popular format for this type of quiz.

A lighter style of quiz format can be built around a popular station personality—the master of ceremonies (MC)—who quizzes volunteer contestants. If the station carries advertising, prizes can be offered by the station's advertisers to winning contestants.

The panel game is a variation on the quiz. It consists of a panel of four personalities under a master of ceremonies who discuss a subject in a light-hearted way. It may take the form of a battle of the sexes with two men and two women on the panel, or it may be a guessing game in which the panel is asked to guess by questioning the identity of an unseen guest who is later interviewed by the MC. Panel games can be highly informative as well as entertaining.

Staging audience programmes

Both the quiz and the panel game before a live audience require systematic, detailed organization.

For an amateur talent quest or lighter quiz the participants should be auditioned before the performance for some people 'freeze up' at a microphone, and this will be evident at the audition.

The audition allows the producer to find out some personal and other facts about the contestants which are later summarized on individual cards for the MC to use in his introductions and interviews.

Where a number of contestants are taking part a special seating plan may need to be worked out so that each participant can be brought to the microphone with a minimum of delay.

The placing of microphones and the seating of the audience must also be given careful consideration. Can every member of the audience see what is happening on stage? How is the audience reaction to be picked up? Does the audience know what it has to do—when to laugh, when to clap?

Most audience participation programmes begin with a 'warm up'. This is not recorded or broadcast but consists simply of some activity on stage to get the audience into a good mood, perhaps funny stories told by the MC.

During the warm up the MC tells the audience what it can do to contribute to the success of the broadcast—he may even have to rehearse the audience laughing or applauding, often necessary if the audience reaction is to be clearly heard.

Audience participation shows must run smoothly without stops and starts and this can only be made possible by good planning and preparation.

Action project

The following was a light programme staged by an African light entertainment producer and produced weekly in a public hall before a live audience. It was a great success with its intended city audience.

If you were the producer how would you go about organizing it? What preliminary planning is necessary? How would you stage it? How would you recruit the contestants? What kinds of microphones would you use and where would you put them? What kind of script would you write for it?

This is an exercise in organization and production.

It was a 30-minute programme titled *Who's Calling?* The MC was a well-known station personality with great talent for ad libbing and making jokes.

The idea behind the programme was simply that four young men each competed in turn for the opportunity to take an attractive and intelligent young woman out to dinner and dancing at a city club at the expense of the radio station.

On stage were two small tables each with a dummy telephone. The tables were separated by a hanging curtain so that the young men and the young woman could not see each other.

Each young man in turn 'telephoned' the girl and tried to convince her by telling tall stories about himself that he was the man of her dreams. She would try by her questions to find out the truth about him; she would also describe what she thought he looked like by his voice and manner.

At the end of the programme the four young men would be brought on stage together and the audience would be asked to vote on who was the most convincing. The MC would briefly interview each young man. The girl then had a 'casting vote' and the two would go off to enjoy the evening,

16

The radio drama

The acting out of a story is an ancient art form that is popular in one form or another all over the world. Sometimes the story is mimed as a dumb-show without words, sometimes it is danced to music and sometimes the story is told in song.

When the story is acted out in words we call it a play and when the play shows how people react when caught up in a conflict we call it drama. Drama with its conflict and suspense is ideally suited to radio.

The story versus the drama

If you wish to understand drama it is important at the outset to understand that a story is not a drama. A story is a mere recital of events. It may be interesting because it is well and colourfully told. It may even hold our interest and give us something to smile about or think about briefly at the end, but we are unlikely to learn anything of substance from it.

The drama on the other hand takes us into the lives and thoughts of people. It shows us their characters and how their characters change and take new directions as a result of the conflicts which face them in their lives and how they win through in the end despite the hazards they have faced.

Drama shows essentially a character in conflict with itself and the fate which he brings upon himself in his struggle to reach the desired end.

Conflict is a universal experience. Because we have all met with conflicts we are able to understand other people. What we want to know in a drama—and what we learn from it—is how other people face up to conflicts.

When the conflicts are inconsequential we have comedy, and when they are profound or deeply disturbing we have the basis of tragedy.

The recital of events which makes a story may end with a moral or a 'twist'. We may have expected it to end one way but it ended another—that is the twist.

In a drama the end is known virtually at the outset of the play but what we are left wanting to know throughout the action of the play is how the end is going to be arrived at. It is the how of the story which makes the action of a play. We must be puzzling all the time as to how it is going to end even if we know that it has only one logical outcome. How a play will end is entirely a matter of the characters in the play and the ways in which they react to things that happen and to one another. Given some happening which interrupts the patterns of our lives we will all react differently. We react differently because our characters are different. A play demonstrates the differences in character and it is this which makes it interesting.

A man may lose his job because of something he has done. What he did was because of his character. How he reacts to the loss of his job will also be a matter of his character. One man may be defiant and threaten his employer with bodily harm and may be arrested by the police for making the threat. Another man may analyse his errors and resolve not to fall prey to them again; he may be reinstated because his employer sees that he has changed his ways. He may also resolve very strongly to correct his ways and may enter into competition with his employer and do better than him. It is all a matter of character.

Some playwrights will take stories which everyone knows—stories which are a part of the national tradition—and use them as vehicles for the analysis of character. William Shakespeare did exactly this and wrote some of the greatest plays of all time. He did not simply tell stories in his plays but used them to display characters in conflict with themselves and with events.

Learning about drama

One of the best ways of learning about drama is to read and study a lot of good plays.

Find out how the author has built up his characters. Analyse them and write down in a few short sentences what kind of people they are, and what happens to them as a result of the action of the play—do they become better or worse?

Discover how the author has built his plot. The plot is all that happens in the play. Most plays have more than one plot; they have several sub-plots. It is the plot and the sub-plot which bring about a change in the direction of the characters.

Notice how the author has all the action of the play take place in full view of the audience. Important action never happens out of sight or out of hearing. We want to see or hear how the characters of the play react to what happens.

Many radio plays have been published. Study these too.

A very good way to learn about radio play writing is to turn published stories or stage plays into radio plays. This is called adapting. If the play is to be broadcast subsequently you must have the permission of the author or his agent.

The radio play

There are three methods of presenting radio plays : (a) as completely self-contained plays of 30, 45 or 60 minutes in length; (b) as serial dramas of 15 or 30 minutes in length in which the action goes forward from one episode to another; (c) as series drama, each broadcast generally lasting for 30 minutes and completing one whole episode of a continued story; the principal characters reappear in new situations in each new drama in the series.

The times include opening and closing presentation—that is announcements and cast credits. Bear in mind that a radio half-hour is usually 29' 30" or 29' 45" to allow time for station identification announcements.

The radio play allows its author and producer rather more freedom than the stage play. The scenery of a radio play is entirely in the listener's imagination and it can be changed frequently if necessary with a few deft words or with sound.

But the radio play also has its restrictions. Too many short scenes with too rapid change of locale and time can confuse the listener. The number of characters in a radio play is generally limited; some radio playwrights believe that seven principal characters should be the maximum. If there are too many characters the listener is constantly wondering: who is speaking now?

All the action in a radio play must be carried in sound. The long silent looks which we may give one another in real life have no place in radio. When the characters in a radio play do things of importance we have to hear them doing them. Read again the chapter on radio writing to be sure you thoroughly understand this.

Where several characters appear in a scene we have to keep them all present. The scene may be a family argument with four or five members of the family present. If the dialogue concerns only two of them for several minutes at a time without the listener hearing any of the others he is likely to wonder where they came from when they do speak. A word or two thrown in here or there, or perhaps a reference to one or more of them will help to keep all the characters present.

The scenes in a good radio play usually end with a strong tag of some kind. It may be a threat or a doubt or a point of view. It is never an inconsequential 'throw away' line. The scenes must end logically but leaving the listener to wonder : what happens now?

Writing the radio play

Assuming you have the germ of a story for a play begin by writing the idea down. If the idea will really support a play you should be able to write down what the play is all about in a few short sentences. This will clarify the idea and point to what is the real action of the play.

It is not sufficient to say, for example, that 'my play is about love'. What kind of love? And in what conditions?

A boy and a girl from two hostile families fall in love. They run away to the city and marry. The marriage is an unhappy one but the unhappiness of the youngsters brings about a reconciliation of the two families.

Writing the idea in this way we find that the real action of the play is not the boy and girl falling in love and running away. Those are only the conditions for the action. The real action is in the reconciliation of the two families and suggests material enough for a powerful drama.

Once you have established the real action you have the material idea for the most important scene. It is called the climax. All the action of the play will build up to this climax and the play will then come rapidly to its end.

Next you have to establish very firmly in your mind the characters of the play. Write down all that you hope to know about them. What they look like, where they come from, what kind of education they have had, how they think and feel, why they think and feel the way they do—and so on. By knowing your characters very well before you start to write the play you will find that when you come to writing it the words and phrases you use will be natural to the characters.

The father of the girl is a gnarled old man of strict views and unforgiving temperament. He is self-centred in his thinking and has always run his household with an unbending will of iron. His sour character developed as a boy when he lost a fight with his neighbour's son who is now the father of the young man. Because he treated his daughter badly and refused to let her attend school she jumped at the first opportunity to get away from home. His daughter . . . etc.

And so on until you have fairly full biographical notes on every leading character in the play. By the time you have done this you will know your characters really well and you may even find them talking to you in your imagination. A very famous playwright once said that he never started writing until he could hear his characters talking to him.

The action of the play then needs to be broken into scenes. This is the stage at which you are plotting your play. The term 'scene' does not necessarily mean the place where the action happens. It is a term for each episode of the play, each section of the action. Each character in a play usually has his own scene; it is a scene he plays with others of course, but it is essentially his. In it he leads the action and reveals something of his character and motives.

By this time you should be in a position to write your play. You know all the characters, you know the climax which is to come and you know the scenes which are going to build up to that climax. All that has to be done is— write.

Where the action is to flow from one setting to another or from one time to another you have before you the problem of effecting a transition. Transitions can be made simply by a narrator. He may say: 'Meanwhile in the city . . .' and lead into another scene. Narrated transitions are, however, best avoided unless the play is more in the nature of a narrative than a dialogue. A better transition might be if the mother of the girl asks in the dialogue: '. . . I wonder what she is doing now?' After a brief pause we may then hear the sound of city traffic followed by the daughter talking. The transition has then been painlessly made.

When you have completed your play you can use your early notes and your delineations of the characters as a synopsis to help the actors in the studio.

A well-written radio play generally provides also a synopsis of the story in a hundred words or so with notes on the various characters with the name of the actor who is to play the part. This is of great help to the actors as it gives them a chance to see at a glance what the play is all about and what character they are playing.

Many other points concerning the writing of your play will be found in the chapter on radio writing.

Sound effects in radio drama

Sound effects can help to heighten the illusion of the radio drama but they are not essential to it. Many great radio plays use no sound effects at all or if they use them they do so only sparingly.

The guiding rule is to use sound effects where they are important to the action or where they help to set the scene.

If a radio play used the sound of people walking every time a character entered or departed from a scene, or for every movement the air would be cluttered with meaningless noise. On the other hand we may need to hear footsteps where, for instance, an important character is a man who limps.

Many sound effects need explaining. A word or two here and there in the dialogue will help the listener to appreciate the sound effect without puzzling as to what it is.

For example:

HE: I put it somewhere . . . now where is it.
[*Effects: Drawer being opened.*]
HE: Oh yes. Here it is.

is somewhat meaningless to the listener. A drawer being opened does not make a particularly characteristic sound. The action needs some explanation if it is to be understood by the listener:

HE: I put it somewhere . . . now where is it. . . . Oh yes!
[*Effects: Drawer being opened.*]
HE: In this drawer.

Many sounds are quite misleading. In some ways this is useful as the producer can manufacture sound effects simply. The cellophane of a cigarette packet crumpled at the microphone sounds like a fire. The striking of a match close to the microphone can sound like a frightening explosion. If the sound of the match is really to sound like a match it needs to be held further back from the microphone and explained in the dialogue:

HE: May I give you a light?
SHE: Thank you . . .
[*Effects: Match struck.*]
SHE [*Draws in breath*].

The words 'a light' and the indrawing of breath make it obvious that the sound is a match.

Sound effects out of place can be used in comedy sequences in light entertainment programmes.

COMIC: What's that? Milk? All right, pour me a glass.
[*Effects: Champagne cork popping. Liquid poured.*]
COMIC: Heady brew. Reminds me of my mother-in-law.

Or again:

COMIC: Right—let's get going. Jump in my car!
[*Effects: Steam train whistle; loud puffs; train starts.*]

Sound effects must be played in the same perspective (see the chapter on getting to know the studio) as the action which takes place around them. They must also be in character.

Let us suppose there is a scene where a mother has a 3-month-old baby in her arms. The baby cries as the mother is talking. The cry must sound as though it is at the same distance from the microphone as the mother's voice, and it must be that of a 3-month-old baby and not a lusty 1-year-old. Again, the footsteps of a young woman walking in high heels must be those of a young woman and not an old man in sandals.

Sound effects must be properly worked out in the script as described under mechanization in the chapter on radio writing.

Sound effects are available on record. They can also be produced live in the studio—these are called manual or spot effects. Many recorded sound effects are unsuitable. For instance, the sound of a telephone bell ringing may not be the sound a telephone makes in your country. The whistle of a train may be different; similarly, the noise of a crowd and so on.

A crowd can easily be simulated with three or four actors. Record them talking—although not actually saying recognizable words—and then play back the recording while having the actors talk again, recording both the play-back and the second lot of talking. This can be repeated several times until you have the size of crowd you need. At each re-take the actors can be at different distances from the microphone.

Casting of drama

This is discussed in the chapter on microphone talent.

In selecting actors remember that their voices must be in keeping with the parts they are to play. Old voices are needed for old people and young voices for young people. It is the sound of the voice not the actual age that counts.

When in doubt about the selection of an actor ask him to visit the studios and audition for you. He can read some lines from the play you have in mind to help you decide whether or not he is suitable. Keep careful notes about his performance and suitability in your talent register.

Indigenous drama

In some African communities there are established theatre parties who travel the countryside from village to village. They seldom work from scripts but generally make up the play as they go along. This is a valid form of drama but is sometimes difficult to use in radio without first teaching the members of the groups something about radio and radio techniques.

The production of these groups for radio is usually a slow process and the play, or parts of it, may need to be recorded several times before it is suitable in radio terms. However it is well worth persevering in such efforts because these groups know a great deal about what the village audience likes and dislikes.

Drama in education

Drama is a powerful vehicle for public instruction.

The series and the serial drama built around popular principal characters can be used for all kinds of teaching. In some countries such serials have run for very many years and have had great influence on the customs of their listeners.

Action projects

1. Select a short story appearing in a magazine or newspaper and adapt it as a short radio play.
2. Discuss with your class the kinds of characters likely to become popular in a series drama which could be used for instructional purposes. What should be the setting for the story?

17

The music programme

Music fills by far the greater part of the broadcast day. It is the letterpress of radio between the news bulletins and featured productions. The general tone and character of a station's music does more to establish the image of a station than any of its other activities.

It is in the nature of all of us to enjoy music. We enjoy it for its rhythms, its melodies and its harmonies. Some music is predominantly melodic—it has memorable tunes—while other music is dominated by its harmonic structure—the way in which notes and groups of notes make pleasant sounds when heard together. European music gives a great deal of emphasis to melody while Indian and Arabic music regards harmony as being more important.

Classification of music

Some authorities classify music under four headings:
1. Primitive music—music with no written score, no known composers and of ancient origin.
2. Folk music—also with no written score but sometimes with known composers; generally of more recent origin.
3. Popular music—sometimes with a written score, composers frequently known, marked melodies.
4. Art music—a written score, composers invariably known, a classical structure.

These classifications of music embrace everything from obscure tribal music to folk ballads, 'top twenty', religious music and the great classical symphonies.

The instruments

The instruments which make music are extremely varied but nearly all over the world different peoples have arrived at similar conclusions, and the instruments of one culture have influenced another.

Some instruments make their sounds by being struck—the water pitcher, the drum, castanets, the strings of the piano. Other instruments move columns of air, such as the saxophone and the organ. A third group makes its sounds by causing strings or strips of metal to vibrate—these are the plucked instruments like the guitar or the African finger piano.

Copyright

The right to reproduce music is known as copyright. It is a system for protecting the composer and in some cases the performer of a piece of music.

Primitive music is never copyright as far as the composer is concerned because the composer is not known. Similarly some folk-music is beyond copyright. But all popular music and art music is subject to copyright. Radio stations pay fees for the use of copyright music.

When copyright music is played on the air, whether live in the studio or from a gramophone record, the details concerning the composer and the publisher and the record manufacturer need to be written down on the station's musical log so that fees rightfully due can be paid. This applies even to music which may be accidentally picked up in the background of an interview recorded outside of the studios.

Information about the owners or controllers of copyrights is printed on the centre label of a gramophone record.

The gramophone library

The gramophone library is the repository for a station s recorded music—music recorded on disc and music recorded on tape. The library should be air conditioned so that the discs and tapes can be stored under the best climatic conditions.

Every radio station indexes its library in some particular way. Every producer who needs music should become thoroughly familiar with the record library, its catalogue and index.

Records and tapes should be handled with care so that they do not become dusty or greasy. They are expensive.

Compiling a music programme

Any musical programme, whether from records or live, must have a form.

The basic form of a musical programme is the unity of material used in it. If it is a programme of popular music it should not stray far from the popular—it may include modern beat groups, album and country and western music. Primitive music and art music would both be out of place in such a programme. Similarly it would be offensive to listeners to an art music programme to include a beat record in it, just as an item of art music would be out of place in a programme of primitive music.

Just as with a talk there is a beginning, a middle and an end so it is with a music programme.

A programme of popular music may open with a number having fast tempo but if we kept up the same tempo throughout the programme it would begin to annoy the listener. After a fast tempo opening, we may follow with something more melodic—a popular romantic vocalist for example. Then a medium-fast number building again to fast tempo and so on through the programme. The final number is generally bright and tuneful.

This variety applies to all music programmes. Even 'top twenty' programmes can be varied by a suitable placement of the various numbers. They do not have to be played in the order in which they appear on the charts.

Presentation

Some radio stations require that the link-continuity in record programmes should be written out or scripted in advance; others allow the announcers or disc-jockeys to ad lib. Where the announcer is ad libbing he should have a good working arrangement with his technical operator who plays the records —a wave of the hand or a nod of the head may be the cue for the operator to start the disc.

Link-continuity should be made interesting. It can tell us something about the artists or the popularity of the number or even compare one rendition with another. But too much talking in a musical programme can annoy the listener; after all he wants to hear the music not the voice.

The announcer who presents many popular disc programmes should familiarize himself with the artists, their careers and what they are currently doing. There are many musical magazines which contain this information.

The production of live music

The live music programme may be made in the studio or outside in a public hall or in a distant village. The music producer of such programmes should know a great deal about microphones and acoustics.

Much that he should know is contained in the earlier relevant chapters discussing the technical facilities of production.

He should have a lively interest in this national music and should seek out new performers. He also has a certain responsibility to research national music and build up a library of it.

Many popular music groups present considerable production problems. Some of them play very loudly—particularly where they use electric guitars —often drowning out the vocalist or vocalists. This problem can often be solved by first recording the instrumental music and then playing it back through earphones to the vocalist who signs into the microphone while listening. His voice and the replayed music tape are mixed and recorded on a single tape. This technique, sometimes called post-dubbing, can produce very fine results. The producer who trains a group to work this way will quickly learn to make high quality productions.

Competitions

National competitions held for periods of several months or a year, prizes and awards being offered by the radio station, can have a marked effect on the standard of live music output. These competitions are often called *eisteddfods* —a Welsh term for the traditional national poetry and music contests. Judging of the competing groups can be divided between a qualified panel and audience reaction.

Competitions which invite audience reaction are also a form of audience research which helps to inform the station about its listeners and their likes and dislikes.

Education by music

When we are young we learn a great deal about life through nursery-rhymes and lullabies. The process of learning through music need not stop simply because we are grown up.

Popular folk-singers can be encouraged to write lyrics which teach village listeners some of the things they should know about diet, hygiene, village government and more lucrative methods of farming. A producer who is interested in this field can obtain the necessary information from the various departments of government concerned with rural development and then work with the folk-singer to develop suitable songs and verses.

Action projects

1. List the musical instruments indigenous to your country and define them as being struck, blown or plucked. Compare these instruments with others which have come from other countries.
2. Select records for a 30-minute music programme of your choice and write the link-continuity.
3. Discuss with your class popular folk-singers who could be used as educators through music. What would you select as the topics which could be most suitably treated in this way? If you have a flair for poetry or song writing, why not try to write a suitable educational ballad.

18

Commercials

Advertising plays an important role in our lives. Just as the news provides us with social and political information, so advertising provides us with commercial information. Social and political information helps us to take a part in the government of our societies while commercial information can be useful to us as individuals and it can force the pace of economic development.

Advertising is not new. The market vendor advertises his wares by displaying them and calling out what he has to offer. A printed cloth draped over a post is an advertisement; so is a collection of clay pitchers, bowls and basins drying in the sun outside the potter's hut.

Many radio stations broadcast advertisements and use the money they make from advertising to finance their programmes. Some have restricted advertising hours and use the advertising revenue as a contribution to their general costs of operation.

Because radio offers a very inexpensive form of advertising it is popular with manufacturers and their agents. By co-operating with their advertisers radio stations can learn a great deal about their audiences for many large advertisers conduct regular surveys on the effectiveness of various media. They can afford to do this much more easily than a radio station and they can also judge from sales which programmes have the greatest pulling power and where the listeners are most numerous.

Radio advertising

A station which carries advertising obtains it either directly from an advertiser or indirectly through an agency representing an advertiser. Where an account is obtained through an agency the agency prepares the advertisements—called copy or commercials—and listens to the station to make sure they are properly broadcast and at the times contracted for. Where a station obtains an account direct from the advertiser the station generally writes the copy.

Radio stations which accept advertising generally offer: (a) time available for sponsorship of complete programmes of any length from 5 minutes to

1 hour; and (b) space or spots of 10, 15, 25, 50 or 100 words or 15, 30 or 60 seconds.

Sponsorships and spots are generally sold in multiples of thirteen. Some stations offer discounts to larger time buyers.

Sponsored programmes can greatly help a station's output of produced programmes as the advertiser pays for the entire costs of production. Public service stations which carry some advertising can increase their production hours by the sale of sponsored programmes. A producer who works on such a station should not overlook the possibility of obtaining sponsorships to enhance his programme output.

Two kinds of advertisements

Some advertisements arrive at the studio as copy to be read by the announcer. This may have been prepared by an advertising agency or by the station's own commercial copy writers.

Other advertisements arrive as production commercials. These are advertisements which have been pre-recorded on tape or disc by the agency or by the station acting on behalf of the agency or the advertiser. Production commercials are sometimes little programmes in themselves—they may use more than one voice and possibly also music and sound effects.

The broadcasting of advertisements

Advertisements must be broadcast at the times stated on the advertising schedule. The cost of advertising may vary at different times of the day. It is generally more expensive at 'peak periods'—the times when more people are considered to be listening. Advertisers sometimes pay an extra loading for their announcements to be broadcast at an exact time such as immediately before or just after a news bulletin.

Where an advertisement is inadvertently dropped from the broadcast schedule a station may have to pay compensation to the advertiser, for example by giving him additional time at no cost.

Some advertisers, particularly those selling patent medicines, like to use 'saturation compaigns'. These are special advertising campaigns in which the name of the product may be broadcast ten or twenty or more times a day. It is a technique sometimes used to introduce a new product to the market. The name of the product may appear in a 'jingle'—that is a tune or a melody.

Writing commercial copy

Writing commercial copy is good training for radio writing of all kinds. Many leading radio and television writers began their careers as commercial copy writers.

Commercial copy writing follows the principles of all good writing. The message must be clear and easily understood. It must inspire the hearer to action. It must also correspond exactly to the time or the number of words which the advertiser has paid for.

Here are some rules for commercial copy writing:

1. Identify the product with the needs and desires of the listener.
2. Avoid negative words and phrases.
3. Use action words and short sentences.
4. Give emphasis to what the listener is expected to do.

We can embody these rules in a twenty-five-word advertisement for a hypothetical make of bicycle: '*Afran*—the bicycle to get you there on time! Avoid crowded buses. Cycle to work on an Afran. Be a *leader*—buy an *inexpensive Afran!*'

We could also write it as a 15-second production commercial.

WOMAN [*calling*]: You'll be late for work, Olu!

MAN: Late? Never. I have my Afran.

WOMAN: Afran?

MAN: Yes—Afran. The bicycle that leads all the way.

WOMAN [*showing interest*]: Afran . . . ? Do they make them for ladies?

MAN: Afran makes bicycles for all the family. [*Close on mike*] There's one for you too! [*Off with emphasis*] Afran!

[*Effects: Sound of bicycle bell.*]

Where an announcer has live commercial copy to read, he should check it to see that it makes sense to the listener.

Station control

Advertising helps the wheels of commerce go around. By stimulating desires it increases the size of the market and the larger the market the cheaper the goods produced for it.

But a station needs to maintain strict control over its advertisers and advertising. The advertisements must not offend good taste, nor be patently untrue. Many stations restrict medical advertising because it can sometimes be misleading. No one has yet invented a pill that cures all known human ailments.

Effective station control of advertising and good salesmanship can convince many advertisers to help carry the costs of public information by sponsorship of important programmes. The audience which the station wants to reach is nearly always the market which the advertiser wants to reach. It is up to the station to show him how.

Action projects

1. Select a number of products advertised in your country and write a number of advertisements for them that would fit into the various word and time spots indicated in this chapter. Remember the writing rules set out in the chapter on radio writing and the additional commercial copy writing rules enumerated in this present chapter.

2. What particular markets are the advertisers you have selected trying to reach? City markets? Country markets? What income groups—the man with a few coins in his pocket, the man with a good income? Where do the advertisers' intended markets and your audiences overlap? Have you programmes which would be good vehicles for those advertisers if your programmes were sponsored?

19

Radio at work with people

The early chapters of this book traced the growth of broadcasting and the evolution of modern programming. Today in many countries the general trend in radio programming has increasingly favoured the news-and-music format—long hours of music, highbrow or lowbrow, interrupted for frequent news bulletins and interspersed with a miscellany of snippets of information.

The new fashion in radio came about as television gained ascendancy over radio as the leading medium of mass communication. It is intended for busy people on the move by day and who, at night, would rather look than listen.

This trend towards music and news programming has spread to radio even in the developing countries often simply so as to follow overseas fashion rather than as a result of any serious evaluation of its worth. In countries which have reached a near-saturation point in television, this use of radio may serve the needs of people but is it appropriate in developing countries? Radio is thus relegated to the background whereas it must be an activity in the foreground if it is to be of any real value in developing countries.

The audience in developing countries

A striking feature of developing countries is the intense interest of people in 'getting ahead' as evidenced by large-scale development plans and by the desire of both men and women for personal advancement. If radio is to be meaningful in these countries it must keep in step with the needs of people; it must ask itself what it can do to help nations—and the men and women who make the nations—to get ahead.

In trying to follow the latest trends in overseas programming, broadcasters run the risk of losing touch with the real needs of their listeners. The sophisticated city man who has spent some years of his life overseas may like his radio as he heard it abroad, but he represents a very small part of the total audience. The radio audience outside the cities is growing rapidly in developing countries and it is this audience which the broadcaster should try to reach.

Getting out amongst people

Broadcasting is more than a studio, a transmitter and a receiving set; it is a communication service. Communication implies a dialogue—a two-way exchange of ideas. The broadcaster cannot work in isolation making programmes for his own satisfaction and simply to earn the flattery of his friends. He is a communicator whose work it is to put one set of people in touch with another.

In any community many people are involved in the educational and developmental processes—community leaders, government servants, teachers, welfare and professional workers. It is the job of the broadcaster to understand the work of these people and show them how to use radio in the public interest. In this respect he has a responsibility to 'sell' radio by demonstrating its usefulness and showing how it can be used.

In the markets and villages

A great deal of a broadcaster's time is spent out of the studios collecting material. This time spent amongst men and women who are his audience provides good opportunities to popularize radio and demonstrate its use.

It may be as simple as showing new listeners how to tune their sets properly and telling them at what times to listen and on what frequencies. Or, he may be able to suggest programmes of particular interest to them— programmes intended for market women or for village farmers.

If he is carrying a tape recorder with him he may be able to produce a programme on the spot—not necessarily intended for broadcasting but simply with the idea of involving people in the use of radio. Perhaps he could arrange for villagers to act out a short play describing their problems. After play-back he may be able to promote some discussion that helps to bring other problems to light—problems of understanding, of interpretation, of listening. If his system has a low-powered district transmitter he may be able to edit and use his material purely for local broadcasting.

From simple activities such as these he will learn a great deal about what radio means to his audience and so broaden his own knowledge of radio as a communications medium.

With the specialists

This 'out of studio' use of radio and its techniques has another place too with the educationists and specialists who are engaged in the daily work of national development.

As a part of their own training and executive programmes, government departments hold many seminars. These seminars provide an excellent opportunity for the broadcaster to get across the message of radio and to offer its facilities to extend the work of specialists. The policeman, the public health worker, the agricultural extension worker, the adult literacy worker are also in the business of communication. They communicate on the more direct personal scale but radio can help give power to their voices and put them more rapidly in touch with a far greater number of people. The broadcaster can show them how to do it.

In teachers' training colleges, large numbers of young men and women are training for the day when they go out into the schools where with blackboard, chalk and radio they will practise their profession. What better opportunity could the schools broadcaster hope to find for teaching the use of radio? He can produce a demonstration programme on the spot and show how it can best be used.

The dedicated broadcaster should seek out every opportunity to involve people in the use of radio. Only by doing this can he forge a real link between radio and its audience.

The opportunities are many

The radio broadcaster in the developing countries has far greater opportunities than his counterpart elsewhere today to make radio a meaningful and effective medium of communication for in those areas of the world radio is the one truly mass medium of communication; it is both needed and respected by its audience. To put it to its proper use the broadcaster must be master of radio techniques, he must know his audience and he must want to use radio for the public good.

Part IV   Staff development and training

20 The problem

The recruitment and training of radio programme staff in Africa faces African broadcasting systems with new problems of a kind that are unknown to broadcasters elsewhere.

In many African countries in recent years the openings for employment have widened enormously and young men and women of the high calibre required for broadcasting find a dazzling array of opportunities facing them in many fields of industry, commerce and government as soon as they leave their schools and universities. Some are attracted to broadcasting but, disappointed with the conditions of service and the limited chances of promotion, they quickly leave to go elsewhere and the broadcasting systems find that they are left with the second best.

Again, some who do remain, particularly at the producer level, are full of ideas and eager to put them into practice but lack the patience to learn the medium first. Often their supervisors do not have the time to work patiently with the newcomers and sometimes the supervisors know very little more about the medium than do the newcomers themselves.

In the older broadcasting systems in the more advanced countries young men and women entering the profession generally have a smattering of everyday technical competence—they are not unfamiliar with gramophones and tape recorders and have ears for high-quality sound—but their counterparts in Africa have not had these opportunities at home to learn the rudiments of their craft. In the African broadcasting systems there is therefore a greater need for some technical training of producers. Again in many of the older broadcasting systems elsewhere it is common practice for young men and women aspiring to become producers to begin as technical operators and they are quite content to remain at this level for a year or so before they move into production. However, the young African with a university degree who is earmarked for production does not take kindly to beginning his career simply as a technical operator; in fact, he tends to reject any attempts to provide him with any technical know-how without realizing that no broadcasting system can function effectively unless its producers are aware of what constitutes technical excellence.

Any training scheme adopted by African broadcasters takes these problems into account.

Recruitment

Broadcasting systems have to advertise their needs if they are to get recruits. They can also foster interest in broadcasting by staging young peoples' programmes which will bring young people into the studios and offer a chance to interest them in broadcasting. Experienced programme officers at the some time have a chance to cull through potential recruits.

In the Unesco survey and report on *Training for Radio and Television in Africa*[1] its authors, Alex Quarmyne of the Ghana Broadcasting Corporation and Francis Bebey of the Division of Development of Mass Communication, Unesco, make the following recommendation: 'African broadcasting organizations should be encouraged to introduce more flexibility into their recruitment processes. This should not be mistaken to mean a lowering of entry requirements. Present standards are suitable but possession of certificates should not be mandatory. The emphases should be on talent, creative ability and an aptitude for broadcasting.'

The emphasis on talent, creative ability and aptitude is all important. Although a broadcasting organization may function as a government department or indeed may be a government department, broadcasting itself is not an administrative or clerical activity. It is show business in which performing ability alone counts. No matter what the programme, it is a performance and it will only hold its audience for as long as it is an attractive or appealing performance.

The authors of the Unesco survey again stress the importance of ability in their recommendation on promotions: 'Broadcasting organizations should be encouraged to recognize and encourage the development of young talent by adopting ability as the main criterion for promotion and proportionately attenuating the importance currently attached to seniority.'

Training

Any training scheme for production personnel in African broadcasting should have the following three objectives:
1. The building of a staff that is technically competent, expert in the techniques of the medium, efficient and responsible.
2. The encouragement of creative and artistic ability.
3. The fostering of understanding of the potential uses of broadcasting for the general economic and social development of the continent.

In regard to this last point the Unesco survey states: 'African broadcasting training programmes should not be limited to the teaching of techniques and the use of equipment. The training should emphasize the utilization of the media in education, agriculture, social welfare and community development.

1. Unesco doc. COM/WS/64.

Every effort should be made to familiarize the trainee with pertinent experiments which have been conducted in various parts of the world, and the necessity of using broadcasting to provide support for development projects should be emphasized.'

Training in broadcasting can be continued throughout the career of a broadcaster as the availability of new equipment makes possible new techniques and as new social developments lead to new programme needs. It is not something to be confined to newcomers only.

Of the various methods of training, the Unesco survey summarizes the views of African broadcasters in the following recommendations.

Basic training. 'As much as possible, African broadcasting organizations should be encouraged to arrange basic formal in-school training in Africa. Equipment in such schools should be comparable in sophistication to facilities normally provided for broadcast purposes.'

On-the-job training. 'On-the-job broadcasting training in Africa is useful and should be continued. However, its many shortcomings must be thoroughly appreciated by African broadcasting organizations. It is most useful if it is utilized only as a familiarization course and not as a complete training course in itself. It is recommended that it should not last more than six months and should commence immediately after recruitment, and be followed with formal training in a broadcasting training school.'

Overseas training. 'As much as possible, training in foreign broadcasting training schools should be limited to advanced level or specialist courses designed for the experienced broadcaster. It presents an opportunity for him to broaden his outlook and at the same time acquire specialist training which is at present not easily available in Africa. . . . Future attachement courses should be limited to experienced senior staff and should not exceed three months. All efforts should be made to secure as many such opportunities as possible.'

The occasional special course. 'Occasional special courses, workshops and seminars should be considered as necessary regular features of broadcasting training schemes. The training of a broadcaster should be envisaged as a continuing process.'

Who has to be trained?

Everyone concerned with the production of radio programmes, newcomers and more experienced broadcasters alike: script typists, production clerical staff; technical operators; microphone talent—announcers, compères and actors and musicians; producers; writers; outside contributors—people who give talks, participate in discussions, conduct religious services; supervisors, heads of programme sections, the programme manager, all require training.

It is a formidable project but unless an effort is made to carry it out, African broadcasting cannot play the role expected of it.

21

The training facilities

The size and scope of training facilities will depend on the size of the station or broadcasting system. A large broadcasting system with several hundred employees will need a whole training wing with several full-time officers, whereas a small station can do little more than delegate to a member of its senior staff some added responsibility for training.

The instructors

Full-time officers should be selected for their experience in a wide range of programming, including experience outside their own broadcasting system. In addition they should have a demonstrated ability to teach and the qualities of leadership.

The larger broadcasting system, which can afford a good training school, should have at least three full-time programme training officers:

One concerned with the training of technical operators and the training of producers in the required technical operation.

One concerned with the training of creative programme workers—producers and outside contributors; writers, actors.

One with a roving commission to supervise on-the-job training and to instruct smaller network stations in the handling of their training problems with regard to technical operators, producers and outside contributors.

In some systems it may also be necessary to have a speech training officer although it may be possible to enlist the co-operation of outside bodies, such as the British Council or the Alliance Française, to undertake this work on behalf of the system.

In addition to its full-time officers, the training facility should be in a position to engage outside lecturers and instructors for specialist courses, general education where needed and lecturers to talk about national history and traditions and national development.

At any level the instructors need to have fairly high grading and executive authority as they will from time to time be called upon to instruct senior officers.

In their supervision of on-the-job training, as distinct from formal courses, instructors or the delegated instructor should sit in on programme meetings, offer criticism of off-air programme checks and arrange a reading programme for station personnel.

The small station

The small station obviously cannot afford or usefully employ a full-time training officer. But it can delegate training responsibility to a senior member of its programme staff.

He should supervise on-the-job training and arrange regular staff seminars. He must do on a small scale what the total training facility is able to do on a larger station.

The facilities

The technical facilities of a training wing should be equal to those of the station itself and contain all the equipment which is in normal daily broadcast use:

A general purpose studio of minimum dimensions—8.75 m × 5.25 m × 3.5 m (ceiling). The studio should be equipped with sound effects materials and at least three microphones.

A production cubicle containing mixing panel, a minimum of two turntables, two tape recorders, and a high quality loudspeaker.

A dubbing and editing suite.

Two class-rooms (one capable of being darkened and used as a theatrette), projection equipment.

A library and reading-room.

A museum of equipment (old and unserviceable) to show students other types of equipment.

The quality of sound throughout the training centre's studios and class-rooms should be first class.

The ideal training centre might also have a hobby room to encourage personnel in manual arts and crafts, photography and so on. If the training centre were linked with an engineering training centre the hobby room could provide facilities for equipment construction and repair. Hobby equipment could be made available at cost.

Where it is not possible to provide a training wing with its own technical facilities the training wing should have access to studios on a regular basis.

In any case the training centre should be made into a lively place which attracts station personnel. It should be the kind of place they want to go to.

22

Some courses

An active programme-production training centre has a full and challenging job as it must considerably influence the development of the station or broadcasting system which it serves. Ideally it should be able to offer courses and appropriate coaching for anyone having anything to do with the programme side of broadcasting—not only staff personnel but also regular and occasional outside contributors. The range of courses which it offers will depend upon the needs of the particular station or system. Here we shall merely draw attention to some essential features.

The induction course is primarily intended to familiarize newcomers with the organization they have entered. It may range in length from three to six weeks depending upon the category of staff. Its purpose should be:

1. To introduce new recruits to broadcasting—its function in the community, its social implications.
2. To familiarize them with the organization they have joined—the conditions of service, the 'where-things-are', the 'whom-to-see' in the staff establishment, the career opportunities, etc.
3. To provide introductory training for the specific jobs they are to do.

Induction courses may embrace many categories of staff simultaneously—clerical and administrative as well as professional—as this can do much to build up the general sense of belonging to a team and to break down the rigid division of staff into otherwise watertight compartments.

Professional couses should begin as soon as is practicable. In cases where a newcomer is called upon to handle expensive technical equipment these courses should begin after a minimum of on-the-job training. The requirements of the various professional courses will vary from one organization to another.

A course for technical operators should in no case be less than thirteen weeks. It may need to be longer depending upon whether technical operators in a given organization are regarded as members of the engineering or the programme division. It should include: basic electricity; studio acoustics; equipment operation; production skills; the role of broadcasting and general science and social studies.

The organization of courses for announcers is generally more difficult as they are few in number. The small station may only be able to train announcers on-the-job by frequent air-checks and regular briefing sessions. Where they are more numerous, regular courses of from six to twelve weeks may be possible. An announcers' course should include: speech work in the languages he uses; the art of programme presentation; compiling the record programme; the writing of link-continuity; the writing of air publicity; news-reading and narration; descriptive outside broadcast commentary; speaking to the microphone; the use of studio equipment; and the role of broadcasting.

Courses for producers must include all the material in this manual and in addition lectures and discussions on national development and over-all social objectives. The producer is, in effect, the editor of a station's output and must therefore be thoroughly conversant with his country and the part which broadcasting has to play in its development.

The best approach to producer training is probably the workshop of from eight to ten weeks duration with heavy emphasis upon practical work in the making of actual programmes. Senior technical operators should attend these workshops as course members as this may lead them into production and will certainly familiarize them with production in a way not practical in day-to-day operation.

An active training centre can back up its producer training by offering short courses of up to a week's duration for script typists and programme executives. These two categories of staff are concerned with actual broadcasting but are frequently overlooked in the training process.

Amongst extension courses which the training centre can run are:

Courses of four weeks duration for supervisors with emphasis upon staff management, critical listening and programme evaluation.

One–subject courses having to do with new social developments, new techniques, new equipment. Such courses may be concerned with sound effects, documentaries, outside-broadcast techniques, etc.

Courses for outsiders may be either part time over several weeks or full time over a week or two. They may be offered to many contributors—potential actors, writers, school-teachers, ministers of religion, government officers concerned with broadcasting. Outside contributors play a large part in the life of a broadcasting station and to a certain extent are its auxiliary staff. They need to learn the techniques of writing for radio and speaking at the microphone.

All practical courses for technical operators, producers and announcers should be fully operational. They should be managed as the station is itself. An operational schedule should be drawn up and strictly adhered to with regard to production time, recording, logging and general administration.

A short reading list

I   *What is broadcasting all about?*

CROZIER, Mary. *Broadcasting, sound and television.* Oxford University Press, 1958.
GREENE, H. Carlton. *The broadcaster's responsibility.* BBC, 1962.
MACKAY, I. *Broadcasting in Nigeria.* Oxford/Ibadan University Press, 1965.
MATHUR, J. C.; NEURATH, Paul. *An Indian experiment in farm radio forums.* Unesco, 1959.
SCHRAMM, Wilbur. *Mass media and national development.* Stanford University/Unesco, 1964.
SILVEY, R. J. E. Methods of listener research employed by the British Broadcasting Corporation. *Journal of the Royal Statistical Society,* vol. CVII, parts iii–iv, 1944.

II   *The technical facilities*

HADDEN, H. *High quality sound production and reproduction.* Iliffe, 1962.
NISBETT, Alec. *The technique of the sound studio.* Focal Press, 1962.
McWILLIAMS, A. A. *Tape recording and reproduction.*
TURNBULL. *Sound effects.*

III   *Radio production*

An African experiment in radio forums for rural development, Ghana 1964/1965. Unesco, 1968. (Reports and papers in mass communication, 51.)
BAILEY, K. V. *The listening schools.* BBC, 1957.
BOOKS, William F. *Radio news editing.* McGraw-Hill, 1948.
CROSS, A. R. *Professional radio writing.* Houghton-Mifflin, 1946.
DUNBAR, Janet. *The radio talk.* Harrap, 1954.
Guide for organisers of radio rural forums. AIR, 1961.
McWHINNIE, Donald. *The art of radio.* Faber, 1959.
MILTON, Ralph. *Radio programming.* Geoffrey Bles, 1968.
Radio broadcasting serves rural development. Unesco, 1965.

IV   *Staff development and training*

GORHAM, Maurice. *Training for radio*. Unesco, 1949.
Professional training for mass communication. Unesco, 1965.

Appendixes

I. AUDITION REPORT SHEET

Name: Sex:

Address: Audition

Phone no.:   date:

Available hours:

Voice age: Character suggested:

Voice quality: Soft   Harsh   Aged fatherly/motherly
               Quiet   Loud   Eager young person
               Throaty   Clear   Formal young person
Diction: Distinct   Indistinct   Timid person
               Slow   Fast   Commanding person
               Natural   Strained   Educated
                                         Uneducated
                                         Other

Ability to sight-read unrehearsed material: poor/fair/good/excellent

What other impressions does the voice give you?

Dramatic ability: poor/fair/good/excellent

Would you say the actor is amenable to direction?   yes/no

How do you grade the actor?   A   B   C   D

---

2. SCRIPT LAYOUT

A radio script is a creative work and a cue control sheet. It should be properly laid out so that it is easy to read and it should contain all information necessary to the production. Here is a form of layout for a dramatic script.

Title:	This is My Land	*Actual duration:*
Sub-title:	The Fisherman's Story	*Tape no.:*
Author:	N. A. Okafor	
Producer:	Bisi Sowande	
Rhearsal:	17.00–20.00 h, 12 February 1971	Studio A
Recording:	20.15–20.45 h, 12 February 1971	Studio A
Transmission:	16.00–16.30 h, 10 March 1971	

Cast:
ANNOUNCER
NARRATOR
OLU THE FISHERMAN—in his late forties; soft spoken; conservative by nature; sense of humour
BISI—OLU's favourite daughter, aged 17/18; light voice which ripples like water
NWANKWO—OLU's cousin; a big energetic man; also a fisherman
IST, 2ND, 3RD VILLAGERS—ANNOUNCER, NARRATOR and NWANKWO can double

Synopsis:
Olu and Nwankwo are close cousins who live in neighbouring villages on the River Ondo. They have long been rivals. Nwankwo comes to visit Olu and they make a bet with each other as to who will catch the most fish. Olu does not know that Nwankwo has newly acquired a long-life nylon net; he loses the bet but learns the value of the new nets.

---

1. ANNOUNCER: 'This is My Land'—a weekly series of programmes telling how progress has come to our villages. Today—'The Fisherman's Story'!
2. [*Panel: Signature tune, 12 seconds. Fade and mix to village background sounds. Hold under.*]
3. NARRATOR: The village of Akibi is a small pleasant village on the banks of the Ondo, a sluggish river, rich in fish, which winds its way slowly to the sea ten miles away. The most respected man of the village is Olu the fisher-man. He sits now in the shade of a tree . . . watching the river . . .
4. [*Effects: Sneak in near-by pounding of yam.*]
5. NARRATOR [*continuing*]: . . . and watching his daughter, Bisi, who pounds yam near by.
6. [*Effects: Swell sound of yam pounding, fade for 7.*]
7. OLU: Who is that coming down the river, child?
8. [*Effects: The pounding stops.*]
9. BISI [*off mike*]: The river, father . . . ?
10. OLU: Yes. Over there . . . in the shade near the far bank . . .
11. BISI [*after a slight pause*]: I think it is our cousin, father—Nwankwo.
12. OLU: I believe you are right, child.
13. NWANKWO [*calling from far off*]: Olu! Olu the fisherman. This is Nwankwo, your rival!
    etc.

3. PERSPECTIVE PLANNING

The chapters 'Getting to Know the Studio' and 'Radio Writing' referred to the importance of perspective planning in the radio drama. It is only through well-planned perspectives and appropriate acoustic environment that the listener can perceive space.

The following short script contains several different perspectives. Can you discover what they are? Write in on the script microphone placings and instructions to the actors which will bring out the various perspectives.

[*Effects: Fade in court-room sounds.*]
CLERK: Pray silence for his Lordship the Supreme Justice! Silence please!
[*Effects/cast: The sound drops substantially.*]
CLERK: Be upstanding for his Lordship.
[*Effects: Movement.*]
[*Effects: Chair moved, footsteps.*]
LORDSHIP [*clears his throat*].
Cast [*small talk*].
[*Effects: Gavel struck.*]
Cast [*talking quietens*].
CLERK: Hear ye, hear ye . . . this court is now in session.
PRISONER: Do you think we have a chance?
LAWYER: A chance? My dear fellow, I'm your counsel. I always have a chance . . . but as for you it's anybody's guess.
LORDSHIP: Thank you Mr. Clerk. Call the first case please.
LAWYER: That's you, my dear fellow. Wish me luck!
PRISONER: Wish *you* luck. It's me who needs the luck.
LAWYER: My dear fellow, if *I* don't have luck, you haven't a chance—so wish me luck, that's all I say.
CLERK: Bring forward the prisoner.
[*Effects/cast: Movement.*]
VOICES: Hang him, hang him! He's a bad man!
[*Effects: Gavel struck.*]
LORDSHIP: Order! At the first sign of a public demonstration I'll have the court cleared!
PROSECUTOR: So you've undertaken to defend him, have you. You haven't got a chance, old man. Not a chance.
LAWYER: I think I have.
PROSECUTOR: In court . . . oh yes, perhaps. But remember how the people feel. Did you hear them call out? They want to see him hanged—and they've got the right judge to do it.
LORDSHIP: Proceed with your opening address, Mr. Prosecutor.
PROSECUTOR: M'Lud. The prosecution's case is simple and direct. The accused was seen to commit the crime by no less than three witnesses one of whom was a senior police officer. Furthermore the prisoner has admitted in a confession taken at the police barracks that he . . .

In planning any perspective effects always ask yourself, where is my microphone? From which point do I want the listener to hear the scene?